WATERLOO TO WELLINGTON

FROM IRON DUKE TO ENLIGHTENED COLLEGE

WATERLOO TO WELLINGTON

From Iron Duke to Enlightened College

JOANNA SELDON

SCALA

Dedication

Semper domus floreat Wellingtoniensis

First published in 2015 by
Scala Arts & Heritage Publishers Ltd
10 Lion Yard · Tremadoc Road · London SW4 7NQ · UK
www.scalapublishers.com

In association with
Wellington College
Crowthorne · Berkshire RG45 7PU · UK
www.wellingtoncollege.org.uk

ISBN 978-1-85759-942-8

Project manager and copy editor: Linda Schofield
Designed and typeset in Brunel by Dalrymple
Printed in China

10 9 8 7 6 5 4 3 2 1

Frontispiece: Sir Thomas Lawrence (1769–1830)
The Duke of Wellington, 1814
Oil on canvas, Apsley House, The Wellington Collection, London
Previous pages: The red-brick Palladian architecture of Wellington College from South Front, 2013

The quotation on pages 122–3 from Queen Victoria's personal diary is by kind permision of the Royal Archives at Windsor (RA VIC/QVJ/1856: 2 June (Princess Beatrice's copies).

Contents

Acknowledgements

This book, published to mark the bicentenary of Waterloo, would not have been possible without the following, to whom I owe enormous thanks: His Grace the 9th Duke of Wellington and Lady Jane Wellesley, who supported the project from the outset; India Ayles, a most intrepid and industrious picture researcher; Felix Cook, our highly capable copyright researcher, College Archives researcher and publicity designer; Oliver Craske, Laura Lappin and Jenny McKinley of Scala Publishers; Robert Dalrymple, for his painstaking work on the book's design; Linda Schofield, my impressively efficient and perceptive editor; Sir Mike Rake and the Governors of Wellington College, in particular Tim Bunting and Peter Mallinson for their generosity in supporting this book; Lucy Atherton and her team in the College Library; Stephen Crouch, Group Finance Director and Bursar of the College; Ben Lewsley, College Archivist; Patrick Mileham, College Historian; Joshua Moses, College Photographer; Adam Rattray, Head of History of Art; Anthony Seldon, 13th Master, who suggested this book be written; Jill Shepherd, Assistant Archivist; Edward Twohig, Director of Art.

The use of the quotation in Chapter III from Queen Victoria's personal diary is by kind permission of the Royal Archives at Windsor.

JOANNA SELDON
Wellington College, November 2014

1 Sunset over the Chapel at Wellington College, 2013

Chronology

2 The battlefield of Waterloo today, showing the Lion's Mound. According to Victor Hugo's *Les Misérables*, Wellington commented, when viewing the mound in 1817, 'They have altered my field of battle.'

1 MAY 1769
Birth of the Hon. Arthur Wesley in Dublin

1781–84
At Eton College

1786
Year at the Equestrian School, Angers, France

MARCH 1787
Enters the army as Ensign

1788
In Ireland as Aide-de-Camp to Lord-Lieutenant

1790
Becomes Member of Parliament for Trim, Ireland

1 FEBRUARY 1793
France declares war on Britain

1793
Proposal of marriage to Kitty Pakenham is rejected

1794–95
In command of a brigade in Flanders

1796–97
En route to India, commanding the 33rd Regiment

1797–1805
In India

1798
Arthur's brother Richard becomes Governor-General of India; family name changes from Wesley to Wellesley.

SEPTEMBER 1803
Battle of Assaye

SEPTEMBER 1804
Awarded Order of the Bath

1805
En route back to England

21 OCTOBER 1805
Battle of Trafalgar

2 DECEMBER 1805
Battle of Austerlitz

APRIL 1806
Becomes Tory Member of Parliament for Rye, East Sussex

10 APRIL 1806
Wedding of Arthur Wellesley and Kitty Pakenham

3 FEBRUARY 1807
Birth of first son, Arthur Richard (later known as Douro)

APRIL 1807
Appointed Chief Secretary of Ireland

1807
Copenhagen expedition. Purchases his horse, Copenhagen

16 JANUARY 1808
Birth of second son, Charles

JULY–AUGUST 1808
En route to Portugal, as temporary commander of expeditionary force

AUGUST 1808
Battle of Roliça; Battle of Vimeiro. Wellesley released from command; Convention of Cintra; Wellesley back in England for the Court of Inquiry.

APRIL 1809
Back in Portugal in command of the defending force

MAY 1809
Wellesley's force crosses the Douro river and captures Oporto

JUNE–JULY 1809
Enters Spain

JULY 1809
Appointed Marshal-General of the Portuguese army

27 JULY 1809
Battle of Talavera

SEPTEMBER 1809
Given the title Viscount Wellington of Talavera. Back in Portugal, Wellington organises the construction of the Lines of Torres Vedras.

JULY 1810
Cuidad Rodrigo, in Spain, surrenders to the French army

SEPTEMBER 1810
Battle of Bussaco, in Portugal

MARCH 1811
Fall of Badajoz, in Spain, to the French army

MAY 1811
Battle of Fuentes de Oñoro; first siege of Badajoz; Almeida, in Portugal, surrenders to Wellington.

MAY–JUNE 1811
Second siege of Badajoz

31 JULY 1811
Promoted to full General

JANUARY 1812
Siege and capture of Cuidad Rodrigo

MARCH–APRIL 1812
Third siege of Badajoz, which is captured by Wellington.

MAY 1812
Lord Liverpool becomes the Tory Prime Minister

JULY 1812
Battle of Salamanca; Wellington enters Madrid.

SEPTEMBER 1812
Becomes Generalissimo of Spanish armies

SEPTEMBER–OCTOBER 1812
Siege of Burgos

DECEMBER 1812
Visits Cadiz and Lisbon, and is given the Portuguese title of Duque da Vitoria

JANUARY 1813
Becomes Colonel of the Royal Regiment of Horse Guards

MARCH 1813
Becomes a Knight of the Garter

JUNE 1813
Battle of Vitoria. Promoted to Field Marshal.

JULY 1813
Battle of the Pyrenees

OCTOBER 1813
Wellington's force crosses the Bidassoa river into France; Pamplona surrenders.

NOVEMBER 1813
Battle of Nivelle

FEBRUARY 1814
Battle of Orthez

MARCH 1814
Treaty of Chaumont; the Allies enter Paris.

APRIL 1814
Napoleon abdicates; Battle of Toulouse ends the Peninsular War; Treaty of Fontainbleau; Louis XVIII returns to France; Napoleon is sent to the island of Elba in the Mediterranean.

MAY 1814
Wellington is made a Duke; first Peace of Paris.

AUGUST 1814
Arrives at the British Embassy in Paris, having been appointed Ambassador to France

FEBRUARY 1815
Arrives in Vienna as the British Plenipotentiary at Congress

MARCH 1815
Napoleon, having escaped from Elba, reaches France

MARCH–JUNE 1815
Wellington leaves the Congress of Vienna to enter the headquarters in Brussels and assemble the Allied army under his control

9 JUNE 1815
Final Act of the Congress of Vienna

15 JUNE 1815
Napoleon crosses the border into Belgium and captures Charleroi; Duchess of Richmond's ball in Brussels.

16 JUNE 1815
Battle of Ligny; Battle of Quatre Bras.

17 JUNE 1815
Prussians retreat to Wavre; Wellington moves to Mont-Saint-Jean.

18 JUNE 1815
Battle of Waterloo

21 JUNE 1815
Wellington crosses the border into France

JULY 1815
Paris surrenders

AUGUST 1815
Napoleon exiled to the island of St Helena in the South Atlantic

OCTOBER 1815
Wellington becomes Commander-in-Chief of the Army of Occupation

FEBRUARY 1816
Wedderburn Webster libel action

JUNE 1816
Attempt to set fire to Wellington's house

FEBRUARY 1818
Cantillon attempts to assassinate Wellington

OCTOBER–NOVEMBER 1818
Congress of Aix-la-Chapelle, leading to the end of the Occupation of France

DECEMBER 1818
Joins Liverpool's Tory Cabinet as Master-General of the Ordnance

AUGUST 1819
Peterloo Massacre

JANUARY 1820
Accession of George IV on the death of George III

FEBRUARY 1820
Cato Street Conspiracy

AUGUST 1820
Trial of Queen Caroline

5 MAY 1821
Death of Napoleon

AUGUST 1822
Accident causes the onset of Wellington's deafness; Lord Castlereagh commits suicide.

OCTOBER–NOVEMBER 1821
Wellington represents Britain at the Congress of Verona

DECEMBER 1824
Defeated by Foreign Minister George Canning on recognition of South American republics

APRIL 1825
Wellington makes plans for Catholic Emancipation

DECEMBER 1825
Financial crisis in Britain

FEBRUARY–APRIL 1826
Wellington on a mission in Russia

DECEMBER 1826
Appointed Constable of the Tower of London

22 JANUARY 1827
Becomes Commander-in-Chief of the army after the death of the Duke of York

FEBRUARY 1827
Prime Minister Lord Liverpool suffers a stroke

APRIL 1827
George Canning becomes Tory Prime Minister; the Tories resign; Wellington refuses to serve under Canning and resigns as Master-General of the Ordnance.

JANUARY 1828
Wellington becomes Prime Minister and so has to resign as Commander-in-Chief

MARCH–MAY 1828
Cabinet in disagreement over the Corn Laws and parliamentary reform

AUGUST 1828
Wellington approaches King George IV regarding the Catholic question

JANUARY 1829
Appointed Lord Warden of the Cinque Ports

FEBRUARY 1828
The Catholic Association is repressed; Tories are split on the question of Emancipation.

MARCH 1829
Wellington fights a duel with the Earl of Winchilsea in Battersea Fields

APRIL 1828
Catholic Emancipation is achieved

JUNE 1829
Accession of William IV on the death of George IV

AUGUST–NOVEMBER 1829
Uprising of agricultural workers under 'Captain Swing'

1830
Wellington refuses to proceed with parliamentary reform; he is defeated in Parliament and resigns as Prime Minister.

APRIL 1831
First Reform Bill fails to be passed

24 APRIL 1831
Death of Kitty Wellington

27 APRIL AND 12 OCTOBER 1831
Apsley House is stoned

OCTOBER 1831
Second Reform Bill is defeated in the House of Lords

MAY 1832
Third Reform Bill is defeated in the House of Lords; much social unrest; Wellington fails to form a government; Earl Grey is recalled as Prime Minister.

7 JUNE 1832
Great Reform Bill becomes law

1833
Wellington is Leader of the House of Lords

1834
Appointed Chancellor of Oxford University

NOVEMBER 1834
William IV dismisses the Whig Government and calls in Wellington, who becomes Prime Minister for 3 weeks

DECEMBER 1834
Wellington refuses to become Prime Minister; appointed Foreign Secretary.

JUNE 1837
Accession of Queen Victoria on the death of William IV

SUMMER 1837
Movement for repeal of the Corn Laws

NOVEMBER 1839 AND FEBRUARY 1840
Wellington suffers severe seizures

1840
Riots in industrial towns

SUMMER 1841
General Election; Robert Peel becomes Prime Minister; Wellington is included in the Cabinet, but without office.

AUGUST 1842
Wellington, from now until his death ten years later, remains Commander-in-Chief of the army

DECEMBER 1845
Supports Peel in the Cabinet split over the repeal of the Corn Laws

JUNE 1846
Corn Bill is passed in the House of Lords

1846
Farewell to party politics

1851
Great Exhibition

14 SEPTEMBER 1852
Death of Wellington at Walmer Castle

18 NOVEMBER 1852
Burial of Wellington at St Paul's Cathedral

LATE 1852
Queen Victoria, Prince Albert and Prime Minister Lord Derby meet to discuss a national memorial to Wellington. Decision made shortly afterwards to found a school for the education of orphaned children of army officers.

AUGUST 1853
Meeting at Buckingham Palace of principal subscribers to the memorial fund

DECEMBER 1853
Wellington College is granted its Royal Charter and Prince Albert is elected the President of the Governors

NOVEMBER 1854
Site for Wellington College chosen

1855
Second Appeal for subscriptions; John Shaw chosen as architect.

2 JUNE 1856
Laying of College's foundation stone by Queen Victoria

MARCH 1858
Appointment of Edward White Benson, later Archbishop of Canterbury, as first Master

20 JANUARY 1859
College opens and first boys arrive

29 JANUARY 1859
Wellington College inaugurated by Queen Victoria

1859
The Wellington magazine first published

31 JULY OR 1 AUGUST 1860
First Speech Day

12 JULY 1861
Laying of Chapel foundation stone following second Speech Day

16 DECEMBER 1861
Death of Prince Albert

16 JULY 1863
Dedication of George Gilbert Scott's Wellington College Chapel

1890
Old Wellingtonian Society founded

8 OCTOBER 1940
Death of Master Robert Longden when the College was bombed

1970S
Girls admitted into the Sixth Form

2005
Decision to move to full co-education

SEPTEMBER 2006
Girls admitted at 13+ and 14+

SEPTEMBER 2008
Introduction of the International Baccalaureate Diploma Programme as an alternative to A Levels in the Sixth Form

2009
Opening of Wellington Academy in Ludgershall, Wiltshire

2012
Opening of Wellington College International in Tianjin, China

2014
Opening of Wellington Primary Academy in Tidworth, Wiltshire

2014
Opening of Wellington College International in Shanghai, China

I have been indebted, in compiling this chronology, to Elizabeth Longford's excellent chronology in her *Wellington: The Years of the Sword* (1969) and *Wellington: Pillar of State* (1972), both published by Weidenfeld & Nicolson.

Introduction

3 Richard Cosway (1742–1821)
Portrait of Arthur Wellesley, later 1st Duke of Wellington, 1808
Watercolour on ivory
Victoria and Albert Museum, London

BORN IN 1769 IN IRELAND, THE THIRD SON OF THE FIRST EARL of Mornington, young Arthur Wesley (this was the family's surname at the time) seemed undistinguished. Judging by his mediocre career at Eton, he looked unlikely to leave a mark on the world. His steady rise to fame, and the flowering of that vital mix of ability – some would call it genius – and relentless hard work, make for an inspiring story. The life of the 1st Duke of Wellington shows a boy without any conspicuous promise developing into a man fêted throughout Europe and commemorated still in place names the world over. He continues to offer a vivid role model, 200 years after the Battle of Waterloo, to the pupils of Wellington College. The school, founded in 1859 by Queen Victoria and the Prince Consort, Albert, as the national memorial to the Duke, gives its pupils the chance to go well beyond expectations and to aim for the heights. This was the Duke's banner for himself and also for those he led.

One of the remarkable things about the Duke is the way in which, after his victory at Waterloo in June 1815, ending the Napoleonic Wars and bringing peace to Europe for 99 years, he continued to play an active role in public life, as Prime Minister and in countless other areas. As the distinguished historian and Old Wellingtonian Sir Michael Howard explains:

> *It fell to Wellington to preside over the restoration of the Bourbons and the enforcement of the new peace ... Waterloo had set him on a pedestal in the eyes of all Europe, but it was his own wisdom that kept him there for thirty-seven more years. The respect and gratitude felt for him, when ... he died in 1852, was no less than it had been when, in 1815, he was greeted as the hero who had banished twenty-five years of nightmare for ever.*

How fitting that Wellington College, the institution named after one of this country's great leaders, now offers its pupils a programme in leadership. The motto inscribed over the entrance to Great School, *Virtutis Fortuna Comes* ('Fortune Favours the Brave'), may be carried by the alumni of Wellington throughout their lives. They will not necessarily follow the Duke in either the military or the public sphere, but will nevertheless show, as he did, courage in all that they undertake. It is to be hoped that they will also share the Duke's strong sense of duty. In his 'Ode on the Death of the Duke of Wellington', Alfred Lord Tennyson, Queen Victoria's poet laureate, declared: 'The path of duty be the way to glory.' These words may grate on the modern ear as a piece of unreconstructed Victoriana, but they are wise nonetheless.

The importance the Duke attached to the idea of service may seem similarly old-fashioned, but it was this concept that moulded his outstanding career. For the 1st Duke of Wellington, whether he was leading a military campaign or His Majesty's government, one principle above all held firm: his chief aim in life was to serve his country. This idea of service lies at the heart of the foundation of Wellington College and continues to be a guiding light for the pupils who follow in the footsteps of this remarkable man.

I hope that pupils currently at Wellington College will continue to read and learn about the exceptional life of the Duke, and about the story of their school. In 1870 the 2nd Duke of Wellington donated his father's Despatches and Parliamentary and Official Papers to the Wellington College library. The next time he visited the College the Duke discovered that none of the pages had been cut: in other words, they had not even been opened, let alone read. 'Your young gentlemen do not seem to have read much of my father's Papers', he observed. If Wellington College continues to flourish as a place of learning, I would like to think that those who are still teenagers as we mark this Waterloo anniversary will show rather more intellectual curiosity than their nineteenth-century predecessors.

4 Francisco de Goya (1746–1828)
Equestrian Portrait of the 1st Duke of Wellington (1769–1852), 1812
Oil on canvas
Apsley House, The Wellington Collection, London

CHAPTER I

The Winner of Waterloo

5 Henry Nelson O'Neil (1817–1880)
Before Waterloo, 1868
Oil on canvas
Private Collection

Described by Queen Victoria as 'the GREATEST man this country has ever produced', the Duke of Wellington was indeed a colossus of his age. It was his military prowess that inspired the founding of a school to honour his memory. So any consideration of the man must start with what it was that made Wellington such a great commander of British and Allied forces during the Napoleonic Wars. What qualities of character and intellect – those very qualities that any great school aims to foster in its pupils – made his campaigns so successful?

First and foremost, of course, Wellington displayed courage of the highest order. The man who claimed 'I am not as afraid of [the French] as everyone else seems to be' was always at the centre of the action, from the Battle of Assaye in India in 1803, where he had a horse killed under him, to Waterloo in 1815 ('the most desperate business I ever was in'), at which he galloped up and down rallying his men. One of these, General Sir Andrew Barnard, later commented: 'We had a notion that while he was there nothing could go wrong.' Perhaps this courage was moulded from the Duke's unpromising childhood as Arthur Wesley, third son in an Anglo-Irish family. His cold and remote mother, Anne, Countess of Mornington, declared 'I vow to God I don't know what I shall do with my awkward son Arthur', concluding that 'he's food for [gun]powder and nothing else', and, seeing him in London for the first time in some years exclaiming 'I do believe that is my ugly boy Arthur.' Such maternal indifference may have developed in this reserved, dreamy violin-playing child a moral courage that, in later years, would prove invaluable.

For a man who had grown up in a relatively loveless environment, however, Wellington – unlike that other great British hero of the

6 Jacques-Louis David (1748–1825)
Unfinished Portrait of General Bonaparte, c.1797–98
Oil on canvas
Musée du Louvre, Paris

Napoleonic Wars (1803–15), Admiral Horatio Nelson – did not court popularity. His courage sprang not from the desire for public acclaim but from the sense, throughout his life, of service and duty. This is why he was always to be found at the fiercest part of a battle: his duty, as he saw it, was to lead by example and take the fire. Wellington's bravery was no more in evidence than at the Battle of Waterloo, where Napoleon Bonaparte's army was larger than his by about twenty thousand men. 'Without his personal exertion, his continued presence wherever and whenever more than usual excitement were recognised, the day had been lost', wrote Colonel Sir Augustus Frazer. When an aide warned Wellington, as they prepared for the final charge to victory at Waterloo, 'we are getting into enclosed ground, and your life is too valuable to throw away', the Duke responded, 'Never mind. Let them fire away. The battle's gained. My life's of no consequence now.'

There can be no doubt that Wellington's bravery arose in part from his relish of a task well done. He even used a metaphor (as others have done) likening battle to sport. Having ousted the French from Portugal in 1809, Wellington was sure he could now tackle them in Spain, writing: 'The ball is now at my foot. And I hope I shall have strength enough to give it a good kick.' After Napoleon's escape from Elba and arrival in Paris in the early spring of 1815, Wellington was given the chance of remaining as British plenipotentiary in Vienna. But of course he preferred the alternative – to become Commander-in-Chief of British forces in the Netherlands. It was not until his exhaustion and distress at the loss of life after Waterloo that he decided the field would no longer be his choice.

One of the most notable aspects of Wellington's courage in battle was that he never delegated, insisting on delivering his orders himself and superintending operations. At Salamanca in 1812, for example, he charged to his brother-in-law, Major General Edward ('Ned') Pakenham, to give orders in person. At Waterloo he rode from one unit to the other all morning, exercising control and inspiring his men with his example. He knew how vital it was to be there. Indeed, it was partly because Napoleon did not share his great rival's practice of delivering orders to his subordinates himself that he lost the Battle of Waterloo, where the emperor's messages were obscure and misleading.

Wellington, however, never took risks. As he wrote to a friend from the Peninsular War in Portugal in 1810: 'They won't draw me from my cautious system ... I'll only fight when I am pretty sure of success.' Two years later he was outlining the same strategy in his communications with the government: he was 'determined ... not to fight an action, unless under very advantageous circumstances, or it should become absolutely necessary.' This customary caution of Wellington's was but another aspect of his courage – the courage to know when to hold back. Throughout the Peninsular campaign (1808–14), he avoided large battles. It was presumably this practice that kept him from moving on 15 June 1815, even after he had been informed that the French forces had driven the Prussians back behind the River Sambre, south of Brussels.

There are other kinds of courage too, of course. For any leader, there is little more fearsome than the press. Wellington, however, was well known for laughing at his treatment by the newspapers. Indeed, one of his most famous aphorisms – 'Publish and be damned' – displays admirable sangfroid in the face of Harriette Wilson's imminent publication of her memoirs in 1824. She was a courtesan who claimed to have had a relationship with him, among others (see plate 7). This is not the place to

7 Unknown artist
The general out-generalled or First come first served, 19th century
Hand-coloured etching
Published by John Duncombe, London
Victoria and Albert Museum, London
Harry R. Beard Collection, given by Isobel Beard

The Duke of Wellington is angry that he is not recognised, while the Duke of Argyll, inside with Harriette Wilson, pretends not to know him.

8 Sir Thomas Lawrence (1769–1830)
Portrait of Catherine, 1st Duchess of Wellington, c.1815
Pencil and chalk
Stratfield Saye

enumerate the various liaisons that Wellington, a married man who relished the company of married ladies, is reputed to have enjoyed. Whether or not such behaviour can be described as courage is questionable and his brave determination to marry Kitty Pakenham having not set eyes on her for ten years may be accounted foolhardy rather than noble (plate 8).

Ambiguities such as these cling to any assessment of Wellington. They are, in part, what has made him such a fascinating subject for biographers. Even his courage in battle, his determination to lead, sprang from a less admirable quality – namely, his inability to trust others. When Lord Uxbridge (later the Marquess of Anglesey), Wellington's second-in-command at Waterloo, enquired about battle plans, his general was less than forthcoming. Obviously, it was explained, everything depended on how and where Napoleon attacked and, as this was the big unknown, no definite plans could be communicated. It was not unreasonable for Uxbridge to have expected more: after all, had Wellington been killed in battle, he would have had to take over command. This incident is typical of the way Wellington behaved even with his confidants. He was the most decisive of men – essential, of course, in any leader. From the Indian campaign (1803) early in his career he learned the importance of making swift decisions, and he never ceased to believe in the value of his own judgement. He had even more reason for this self-belief after the Peninsular War, for he now had greater experience than any other general when it came to fighting the French. It is the Peninsula, rather than Waterloo, that can be counted as Wellington's major triumph of military strategy.

Although his strengths often lay in remaining on the defensive – and indeed there were those who claimed that he prolonged hostilities by being too cautious – the Peninsular War showed that he knew exactly when to attack. Salamanca (1812) was the first big battle of the campaign in which Wellington took the offensive on his own initiative (plate 9). Earlier, the course of the Battle of Talavera in 1809 had confirmed his sense that victory was unlikely if he was not there to control everything. To Prime Minister Lord Liverpool he wrote, 'I am obliged to be everywhere, and if absent from any operation, something goes wrong.' He always knew his own mind and stood by his decisions, even when others disagreed with him. At the close of 1810, for example, despite the fact that Wellington's Anglo-Portuguese army was steadily pushing the French back towards Spain, there were many in Britain, including the Prince of Wales, who felt that peace should be made with Napoleon. Needless to say, this was not a view shared by Wellington. As his aide-de-camp Lieutenant-Colonel Sir Alexander Gordon exclaimed: 'Thank God Wellington is not a man to be moved by popular clamour.'

9 Cecil Langley Doughty (1913–1985)
With the Iron Duke at Salamanca, 20th century
Colour lithograph
Private Collection

When the moment for action came, he recognised it immediately. Wellington's decision in the small hours of 16 June, two days before the battle, to fight Napoleon at Waterloo, was, according to military historian and Old Wellingtonian Peter Snow, 'perhaps the most singular example of how he was able to make a colossal decision with such cool confidence'. In the early evening of 18 June, as the Battle of Waterloo reached its turning point and Wellington saw Napoleon's elite Imperial Guard in retreat, his triumphantly decisive 'Oh dammit, in for a penny, in for a pound' launched the allied armies' final pursuit of the French and sealed the end of 12 years of war in Europe.

So perhaps one could argue that decisiveness tended to go hand in hand with an inability to trust people. This is the man, remember, who charged all over the battlefield himself, rather than confiding his orders to anyone else. As military historian Richard Holmes has remarked: he had 'the symptoms of what we would now term a control freak'. This is well exemplified in Wellington's furious response when Sir James

McGrigor, his chief medical officer in the Peninsula, told him that, contrary to the general's orders, he had redirected the route of the sick and injured to field hospitals. Wellington was sitting for his portrait by Goya at the time: perhaps McGrigor's objectionable initiative accounts for the expression on the sitter's face (see plate 34). Arguably, however, Wellington was correct to take all the decisions himself. According to the memoirs he wrote on St Helena, Napoleon was eventually defeated partly because his commanders tended to take matters into their own hands. In 1801, in his early 30s and awaiting recognition, Wellington (still Wellesley at the time) wrote to his brother Henry, 'I like to walk alone'. Independent judgement, and the loneliness that attends it, seem to have been integral to his character.

10 George Abbott (1803–1883) *Arthur Wellesley, 1st Duke of Wellington (1769–1852) Field-Marshal & Prime Minister*, c.1862
Copeland Parian figure
British Embassy, Paris

In the end, autocratic decision-making and a reluctance to delegate matter little if a leader has the complete trust of his followers. A young Swiss officer who encountered Wellington in the Peninsula commented on the complete confidence in which he was held by the army: 'I have heard him – wrongly, I think – accused of hauteur.' But a revealing anecdote is recounted in Field Marshal Viscount Montgomery's *A History of Warfare*: Winston Churchill told Montgomery that a friend once asked the Duke, by then very old, if there was anything he would do better if he had his life over again. And Wellington replied, 'Yes, I should have given more praise.'

Hand in hand with this physical courage and moral confidence in his own judgement went Wellington's ability to stay calm under pressure. This quality – mentioned repeatedly by his military colleagues – is of course another mark of a true leader and goes some way to explaining the man's greatness. Colonel Campbell of the 78th Highlanders, describing Wellington at the Battle of Assaye in 1803, commented: 'The General was in the thick of the action the whole time... I never saw a man so cool and collected.' At Talavera, as new French infantry swarmed in through a gap in the British line, it was Wellington's calm that saved the day. He swiftly organised for the gaps to be filled and after fierce fighting the French withdrew.

One way in which Wellington maintained an even mental keel was to allow himself time to do things he enjoyed, even in the middle of a campaign. A favourite pastime was hunting. There is a story that on one occasion during the Peninsular War some greyhounds passed close to him, chasing a hare, just as he was preparing to fight. As soon as he saw them, off he went in hot pursuit, returning to do battle renewed and refreshed. It was doubtless because Wellington's fondness for hunting was well known that Lieutenant Howell Rees Gronow, describing the Duke setting off for Waterloo with his fellow officers, claimed: 'They all seemed as gay and unconcerned as if they were riding to meet the hounds in some quiet English country.'

The most famous proof of Wellington's calm self-possession is to be found in the events surrounding the Duchess of Richmond's ball. In the build-up to Waterloo, even when Napoleon's invasion seemed imminent, high society flocked to the Brussels war zone. War has always had its camp followers, and among these were some very fine ladies, including Lady Frances Wedderburn Webster, the wife of an army officer and a former lover of Lord Byron, who at the time was involved in a relationship with the Duke. Wellington was keen to preserve the party atmosphere in Brussels as a cover for the allied army he was gathering against the French. So when the Duchess of Richmond, who planned to hold a ball in her rented home in Brussels on 15 June, asked permission for the event to go ahead, the great man's answer was 'yes', by all means. Wellington

11 Robert Alexander Hillingford (1828–1904)
The Duchess of Richmond's Ball, 1870s
Oil on canvas
Goodwood House, Chichester

12 John Everett Millais (1829–1898)
The Black Brunswickers, 1860
Oil on canvas
Lady Lever Art Gallery, Port Sunlight
Notice Jacques-Louis David's equestrian portrait of Napoleon in the background.

knew that a sure-fire way of maintaining calm would be the issuing of invitations to a ball.

Just before midnight, when the ball was at its height, Wellington was informed that Napoleon's army was proceeding north from Charleroi. The enemy was moving fast and Wellington had been caught off guard: 'Napoleon has humbugged me, by God! He has gained twenty-four hours' march on me.' These were his words to his host just before leaving the ball. The story goes that he then asked the Duke of Richmond if he had a map. Examining it, he observed that, although he had ordered his army to try to stop Napoleon at the Quatre Bras crossroads, 'we shall not stop there, and if so, I must fight him here.' So saying, he placed his thumbnail over the place we now all know as Waterloo. Still cool and collected, he set off early the next morning, having quietly informed his officers (almost all present at the ball, of course) of what they needed to do.

Little wonder, then, that Wellington was viewed as a hero by so many, in a way not very different from the status of national saviour accorded to Winston Churchill after the Second World War. Even the Prince Regent was effusive, writing to Wellington in July 1813 to congratulate him on his victory at Vitoria (which marked the beginning of the end for the French in Spain), and to confer on him the office of Field Marshal and the title of Marquess: 'Your glorious conduct is beyond all human praise, and far beyond my reward. I know no language the world affords worthy to express it. I ... devoutly offer up my prayer of gratitude to Providence, that it has ... blessed my country and myself with such a General.' Ludwig van Beethoven composed 'Wellington's Victory' in honour of Vitoria: this included the 'Rule Britannia' theme and 'For He's a Jolly Good Fellow'

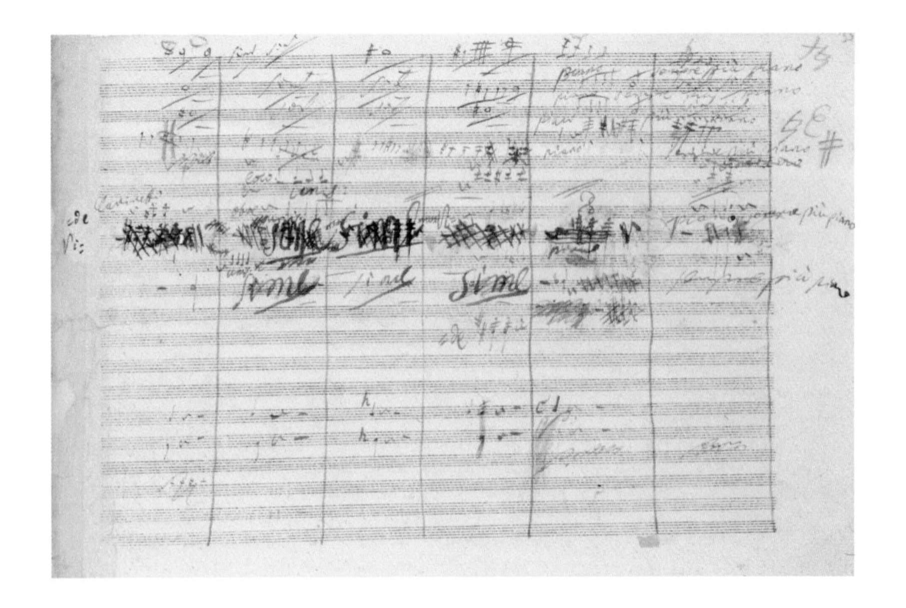

13 Ludwig van Beethoven (1770–1827)
'Wellington's Victory Op. 91', page 36, 19th century
Pen and ink on paper
Staatsbibliothek, Berlin

14 James Ward RA
(1769–1859)
Copenhagen, The Horse Ridden by the Duke of Wellington at the Battle of Waterloo, c.1824
Lithograph
National Army Museum, London

(of which there is a German version). A contemporary letter described the Duke as the troops' 'idol'. As Wellington himself observed, the soldiers 'will do for me what perhaps no one else can make them do'. So it is not surprising that, on hearing news of Napoleon's escape from Elba early in 1815, Tsar Alexander, placing his hand on Wellington's shoulder when they met in Vienna (where the latter was British plenipotentiary), declared: 'It is for you to save the world again.'

The public loved Wellington. After his victory at Salamanca the locals cut pieces off the skirts of his coat to keep as relics. When he returned home from the Peninsula for the first time in five years, crowds following his coach all the way from Dover to London, he was practically carried by his admirers for the final part of the journey – until he managed to get onto a horse and ride back alone. Eyewitness accounts by those who served alongside him simmer with the ecstasy of those who have been fortunate enough to rub shoulders with a demigod. After Waterloo, naturally, his heroic status soared higher still, and George Friedrich Handel's 'See the Conquering Hero Comes' greeted him everywhere. It is hardly surprising, then, that so many streets, squares and pubs, and a city in New Zealand, are named after him.

Although Wellington was admired rather than loved by his men, they did have an affectionate nickname for him, thanks to his most distinctive facial feature. 'Glorious news!' wrote Private Wheeler in an 1815 letter, 'Nosey has got command! Won't we give them a drubbing now!' And John Kincaid, one of Wellington's officers, confessed, 'We would rather see his long nose in the fight than a reinforcement of ten thousand men any day.' (see plate 15)

One of the reasons the men respected him must have been that, despite the adulation in which he was held, Wellington was never ostentatious. Wishing to avoid the clichéd trappings of the military commander, his chosen instrument on the battlefield was the telescope. He was frequently to be found with this fixed to his eye as he surveyed and assessed the position. Dissatisfied when Sir Thomas Lawrence painted him with a watch in his hand, he insisted: 'I was *not* waiting for the arrival of the Prussians at Waterloo. Put a telescope in my hand, if you please.' (Lawrence's portrait of the Duke, with what looks like a somewhat over-scaled wooden and brass telescope at his shoulder, hangs to this day at Wellington College (plate 16). Instead of scarlet and gold braid, he chose to wear a blue frock coat – and, of course, those special boots, shorter and more loosely fitted than modern riding boots, sometimes worn with leather mudguards. Waiting for Napoleon to attack in 1815, he took delivery of two pairs of 'Wellingtons' specially made for the campaign by his London boot-maker (plate 17).

When Wellington entered Paris in May 1814 after Napoleon's abdication (see plate 18) and his own elevation to Duke, he and Spanish General Miguel de Alava offered celebratory toasts. Wellington was congratulated in several languages and cheered for nearly ten minutes. According to an eyewitness, the Duke 'bowed, confused, and immediately asked for coffee'. He was genuinely modest. When in 1808 he visited Lisbon, whose citizens wanted to give him the red carpet treatment, he decided, 'I will arrive at Lisbon in the dark so there must be no ceremony.' Commenting on how well received he had been in Cadiz and Lisbon in January 1813, he added, 'I ought to have somebody behind me to remind me that I am "but a man".' He was always alert to the perils of the pedestal. Writing to Lady Salisbury more than 20 years later, he echoed his earlier remark: 'I feel I am but a man.' The diarist Charles Greville commented that Wellington's greatness was the result of 'a few striking qualities – a perfect simplicity of character, without a particle of vanity or conceit, but with a thorough and strenuous self-reliance, a severe truthfulness, never misled by fancy or exaggeration'.

Another reason for Wellington's success – as indeed it is for any great leader – was his personal self-discipline. This may be accounted for in part by his experience as a young man of being rejected by Lord Longford as a suitor for his daughter Kitty Pakenham. Arthur Wesley (as he then

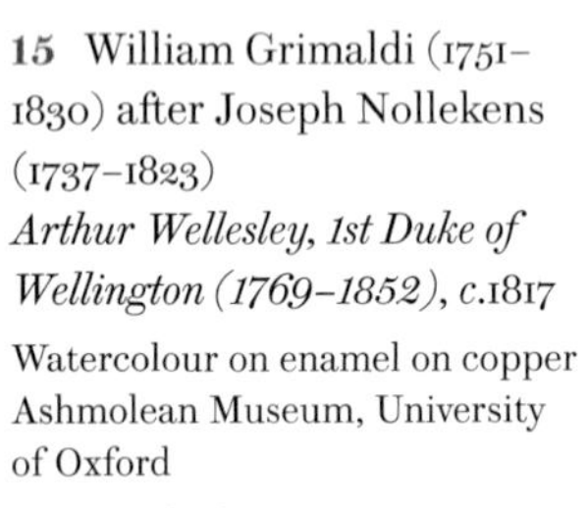

15 William Grimaldi (1751–1830) after Joseph Nollekens (1737–1823)
Arthur Wellesley, 1st Duke of Wellington (1769–1852), c.1817
Watercolour on enamel on copper
Ashmolean Museum, University of Oxford
Trompe l'oeil cameo portrait miniature of a marble bust, profile to the right.

16 Sir Thomas Lawrence (1769–1830)
Arthur Wellesley, Duke of Wellington, with a telescope, 1828
Oil on canvas
Wellington College

17 Wellington's boots, *c.*1817
Walmer Castle

18 Paul Delaroche (1797–1856)
Napoleon (1769–1821) after his Abdication, 19th century
Oil on canvas
Musée de l'Armée, Paris

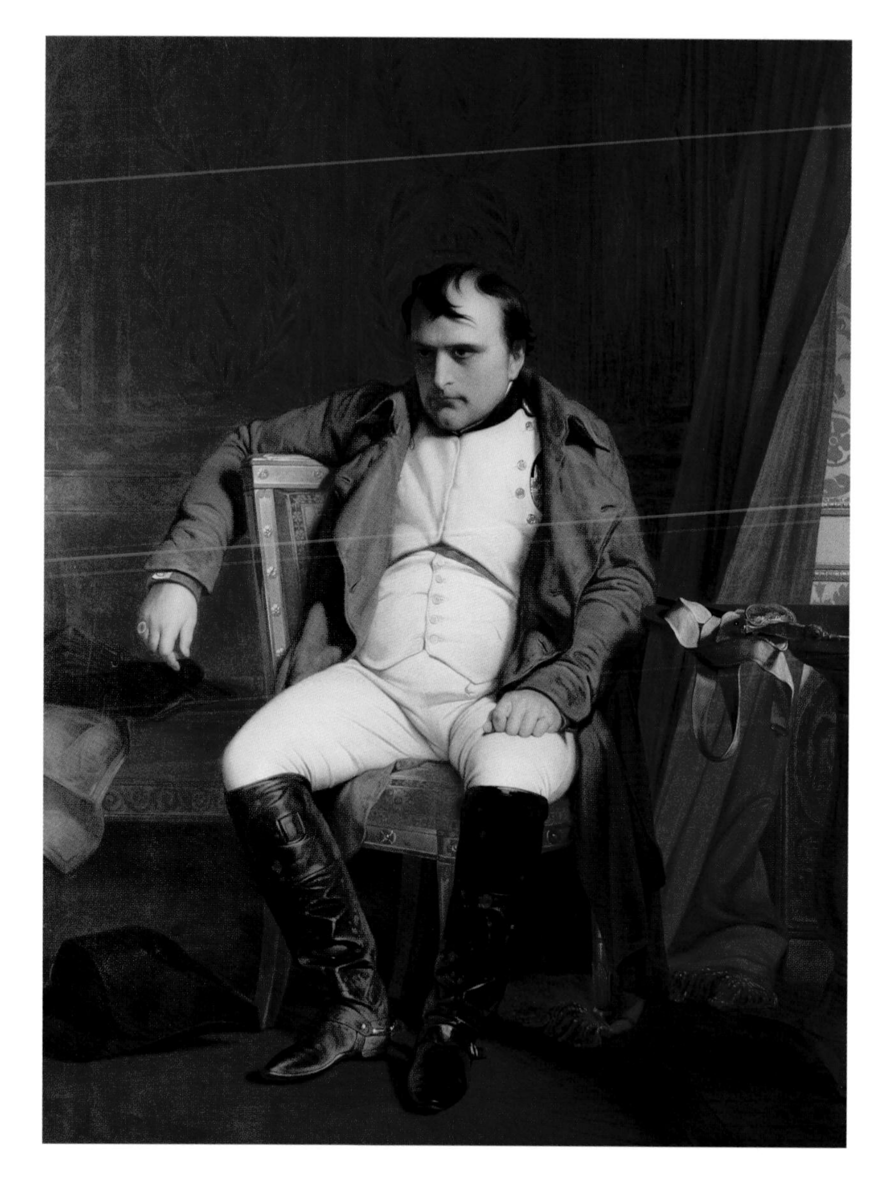

was) determined immediately that he would excel in his military career and so win the hand of the woman on whom he had fixed his heart. To this end, in the summer of 1793 he burned his violin – a chief companion and solace of his childhood – vowing to play no more and to set his sights on worldly success. He joined the war against revolutionary France as a commander in the Netherlands. There are few motives stronger than wounded pride in driving a man to be severe with himself in his habits.

Indeed, Wellington's habits were both revealing and exemplary. He certainly kept himself in good shape, with the result that the actress Marguerite-Josephine Weimar (plate 20), who claimed to have slept with both Napoleon and Wellington, declared that 'M. le Duc était

de beaucoup le plus fort'. Once married, the Duke and Kitty were, sadly, disappointed and one of le duc's less admirable habits was exercised with married ladies. He relished beauty, but spurned luxury. Wellington's campaign headquarters were as lacking in flamboyance as his dress. Sometimes he lodged in quarters, but, when necessary, was happy to stay in a large tent. If he thought the enemy might be on the move, he would sleep, according to Lieutenant Thomas Browne, 'in his clothes with his boots near him ... His horse and that of his orderly dragoons were always ready saddled'. His routine may be contrasted with that of his opposite number in Portugal, the French Marshal Soult, as Wellington prepared to cross the River Douro and so reach Oporto in 1809. While Soult, having been up all night working, went to bed and allowed his men a prolonged breakfast, Wellington was up early with his telescope making plans from a hilltop. At 11.30am Soult was awoken to be told that the British had crossed the river. By teatime Wellington had taken over Soult's villa and was enjoying the Frenchman's uneaten lunch. But he certainly was not one for whom gourmet food was important. His normal breakfast consisted of tea and toast. He drank considerably less than was fashionable at the time and his favourite food was roast mutton. His 5pm dinners were renowned as both generous and informal.

19 Sir Thomas Lawrence (1769–1830)
Arthur Wellesley, 1st Duke of Wellington, 1814–15
Oil on canvas
Royal Collection, London

20 After Rose Emma Drummond (active 1815–1837)
Mademoiselle Georges (Marguerite-Josephine Weimer), 1817
Stipple engraving
Published by John Bell, 1817
National Portrait Gallery, London
'Monsieur le Duc était de beaucoup le plus fort' (The Duke was much the stronger) was her assessment of Wellington's prowess in comparison to Napoleon's.

21 Honoré Daumier (1808–1879)
Nicolas Soult, Marshal of France, 1832
Unbaked clay
Musée d'Orsay, Paris

Wellington's capacity to perform at a high level on very little sleep offers another clue to his success. Over a fortnight in July 1812 he spent less than 48 hours in bed. On the night of 15 June 1815, before marching towards Quatre Bras (the night of the famous ball), he had less than two hours' sleep. On the following night he had about three hours' sleep, and then on the night before Waterloo itself he managed just another three hours. The battle was over, but there was still little chance to rest. Leaving behind his dead and wounded friends, and with a total of about ten hours' sleep in four nights, he rode back to Brussels and immediately wrote to the Earl of Aberdeen, commiserating on the death of his brother, Wellington's aide-de-camp Alexander Gordon, and adding, with an impressive memory and eye for detail, that Gordon had 'a black horse, given to him, I believe, by Lord Ashburnham, which I will keep till I hear from you what you wish should be done with it.' Wellington naturally received a huge amount of correspondence. Another aspect of his rigid routine was his determination to answer letters as soon as they arrived.

Wellington was indeed what we would now call a workaholic. He took no home leave between spring 1809 and summer 1814 (perhaps a function, also, of his unhappy marriage). He was serious-minded and, in

previous pages

22 Joseph Mallord William Turner (1775–1851)
The Field of Waterloo, exhibited 1818
Oil on canvas
Tate, London

23 After Paul Alexandre Protais (1826–1890)
After the Battle – A Corner of the Field of Waterloo, c.1850
Photogravure
Printed by Gebbie & Husson Co. Ltd
McGill University, Montreal

keeping with the aspirations of the period, keen on self-improvement. When he sailed to India in 1796, he took with him a library of books he had purchased recently. These included titles focused specifically on the sub-continent, for example Quintin Crauford's *Sketches of the Hindoos* (1792) and Warren Hastings's *Memoirs of Bengal*, and seminal works of politics and economy such as any well-educated man would be expected to have read: Plutarch's *Lives* (all six volumes, 1517), Adam Smith's *The Wealth of Nations* (three volumes, 1776) and the 24-volume works of Jonathan Swift. This was the young man who failed to distinguish himself as a pupil at Eton.

But Wellington had his lighter side too, and was certainly sociable. He always enjoyed a good party. It was not just to maintain a calm atmosphere that he attended the Duchess of Richmond's ball in Brussels. After leaving school he had gone to study at the French Equestrian School at Angers and there he learned how to dance. In an 1804 letter to Mrs Gurdon, he wrote from Bombay, 'the floor of my tent is in a fine state for dancing and the fiddlers of the Dragoons and 78th and Bagpipes of the 74th play delightfully.' Part of his skill as a leader was an understanding of human psychology and ensuring that morale was kept high by events such as these.

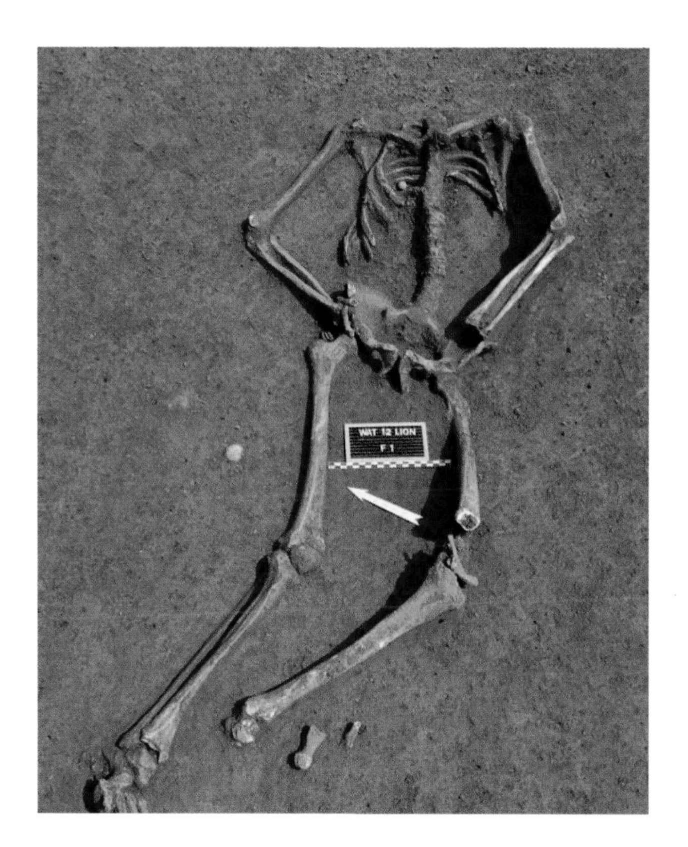

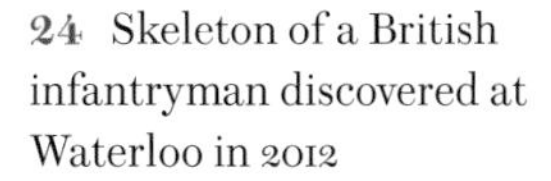
24 Skeleton of a British infantryman discovered at Waterloo in 2012

Above all, however, Wellington's military achievements can be explained by his skills as a strategist. In later life he claimed that his 'spirit of enterprise' was formed at Eton and 'the tricks I used to play in the garden' there. He used a vivid image to distinguish his approach to military strategy from that of his opponents. 'They planned their campaigns just as you might make a splendid piece of harness. It looks very well; and answers very well; until it gets broken; and then you are done for. Now I make my campaigns of ropes. If anything went wrong, I tied a knot; and went on.' Undoubtedly his time in Angers helped him to understand the French model. On his Indian campaign (1803–5) he built up his ideas on tactics. These were then put into practice in the Peninsular War. From as early as May 1808, Wellington recognised that, by diverting Napoleon's forces away from other parts of Europe and into Spain and Portugal, he would be doing much to sap the emperor's strength. Wellington's dogged snapping at Napoleon's western ankles meant that French energies and attention were being pulled in too many directions ever to be wholly effective. This undoubtedly marked the turning point of the Napoleonic Wars. Wherever possible on the Peninsula, Wellington tried to keep the French forces divided, thus enabling him to pick them off one by one.

In keeping with his 'knotted rope' metaphor, Wellington's strategy – sometimes at its most effective at short notice – exploited the element of surprise. In one of his early Portuguese battles – Vimeiro, in 1808

25 After Benjamin Robert Haydon (1786–1846)
Field Marshal Sir Arthur Wellesley (1769–1852), 1st Duke of Wellington, as an Old Man Surveying the Battlefield of Waterloo, c.1840
Oil on canvas
National Army Museum, London

– he placed 800 men in two ranks firing muskets at the approaching French columns at very close range: 'I received them in line, which they were not accustomed to.' Another instance of Wellington's cunning was in the build-up to the Battle of Oporto in 1809: he gave the go-ahead ('Well, let the men cross') for British troops to be ferried across the River Douro in four barges used by the Portuguese to carry the local wine over. Later in 1809, at the Battle of Talavera, he divided his army into four units – divisions, brigades, battalions and companies. Six years later at Waterloo, as Snow has pointed out, Wellington was still using this structure. Gradually, the French commanders – but, significantly, not Napoleon himself, who never went to the Peninsula – recognised that their enemy was formidable. General Maximilien Foy, after fighting Wellington at Salamanca three years later, remarked on 'his prudence, his eye for choosing a position, and his skill in utilising it.' Calling him a 'master of manoeuvres', he even went so far as to compare him to the Duke of Marlborough and Frederick the Great.

Wellington recognised how important it was to move with stealth. Captain Sir John Kincaid, who witnessed the capture of Ciudad Rodrigo in January 1812, claimed that Wellington achieved this 'by a combination of secrecy, audacity and speed ... He hid his preparations beneath a veil of profoundest silence and mystery'. During the following month, Wellington acted as inconspicuously as possible in sending the allied army towards Badajoz, making sure he remained at Cuidad Rodrigo to put the enemy off the scent. At Vitoria, the 1813 battle that finally wrested Spain from Napoleon, Wellington correctly guessed that the French would anticipate an assault from the west: surprise and stealth were once again his key tactics, and he therefore made to attack General Betrand Clausel from four different directions. His opponent was left reeling.

Wellington's clever preparations for battle, and his flexibility in changing his plans as the need arose, were qualities he could use off the battlefield as well. His decision to give the go-ahead to the Duchess of Richmond's pre-Waterloo ball was wholly characteristic of a man who liked to scatter red herrings, misleading the enemy as to his intentions. After all, it made sense to hold a large social event. As Lord Fitzroy Somerset observed in a *Waterloo Memorandum*, the ball was 'the place where every British officer of rank was likely to be found; perhaps for that reason the Duke dressed and went there.' How easy, then, to give orders when it was time to march. In the meantime, and before committing his troops in a particular direction, Wellington had a chance to find out precisely where Napoleon would attack (see plate 5).

In the encounter at Quatre Bras, two days before the Battle of Waterloo, Wellington continued to play a waiting game. He put his

BATTLE:OF:VITTORIA:GAINED:JUNE:21:AD:18

26 Thomas Stothard (1755–1834)
Detail from the Wellington Shield, 1822
Silver-gilt
Apsley House, The Wellington Collection, London

forces in key positions, where they stood with their muskets, secure and ready for the French attack. As in the Peninsula, they were therefore well placed to inflict high casualties on the advancing columns. Wellington was up early the following day, relying on his knowledge of Napoleon's habits – in particular that of giving his troops an early night and a lie-in after a big battle. Too late, the emperor realised he should have moved more quickly. This strategic brilliance continued at Waterloo itself where, despite setbacks, Wellington recognised that keeping the French out of Hougoumont was vital (plate 27). Once again, he relied on the tactic of stealth, at this stage keeping his men invisible behind the top of a ridge. Wellington's frequently defensive tactics were, arguably, a subtle form of gamesmanship.

One essential ingredient of Wellington's military genius was his understanding and exploitation of topography. An early example of this is found at Assaye, where, viewing two villages on opposite banks of the River Kaitna, he 'immediately said to myself that men could not have built two villages so close to one another ... without some habitual means

27 Robert Gibb (1845–1932)
Closing the Gates at Hougoumont, 1815, 1903
Oil on canvas
National Museums Scotland

of communication.' He insisted there must be a ford, which the officer he sent on ahead duly found. Thanks to this blend of inspiration and plain common sense, he was able to lead his army across the ford and into battle on favourable ground.

Even when not directly planning a battle, he had an eye for the significance of a terrain. One of Wellington's greatest coups was the creation of the Lines of Torres Vedras, which emerged from his assessment of the contours of the hills north of Lisbon through which the French army would have to make their way to the Portuguese capital. The Lines were groups of hill forts along a 30-mile stretch commanding all routes. Constructed under the supervision of his chief engineer, Colonel Richard Fletcher, these three lines of redoubts, parapets and ditches covered

28 Charles Turner (1774–1857) after Thomas Staunton St Clair (1785–1846)
A View of the Serra de Busacco at San Antonio de Cantara Showing the Attack by Marshal Reigniers Upon the British and Portuguese Forces Under Lt. General Sir Thomas Picton, 27th September 1810, 1815
Engraving
Private Collection

a considerable segment of Portugal between the River Tagus and the sea. Perhaps the battle in the Peninsula that most clearly exemplified Wellington's understanding of the terrain was Salamanca, where much of the fighting centred on the control of two hills. The British occupied the Lesser Arapil, but he knew it was crucial to capture the Greater Arapil from the enemy, and focused his battle plan – which included tricking Marshal Marmont as to the direction in which his forces were moving – to this end.

A chief feature of Wellington's skilful use of topography was his fondness for concealing his forces behind hills – for example at Rolica and at Vimeiro in 1808. Positioning his troops for Talavera, he kept most of the

29th Infantry Regiment behind a hill on the reverse slope, so the French would not see them. The men were to work their way behind the brow of the hill and lie flat on the ground. As soon as they had the advantage, they were ordered to fire, and then charge. At Waterloo, also, Wellington saw a perfect opportunity in the ridge's reverse slope, where he placed most of his infantry the evening before the battle. During the fighting itself, he used his habitual reverse slope tactic, with its vital element of surprise.

Wellington's eye for the potential of terrain may be contrasted with that of his French opposite number between 1809 and 1811. Marshal André Masséna (whom Wellington admired) was ill-equipped to meet his opponents at Bussaco in 1810, having been misled by poor maps and guides (plate 28). 'There are certainly many bad roads in Portugal', observed Wellington, 'but the enemy has taken decidedly the worst in the whole kingdom'. The French force was going to have to struggle through the steep, rocky slopes of Bussaco, a mountain ridge from which Wellington gazed down, tracking every step Masséna's men took. The French commander, at this moment at least, did not show any talent for topography, deciding to launch an attack on an enemy who could quite clearly see him coming.

Any good soldier has to be practical. Wellington was more than this: he was meticulous down to the smallest detail. It was Napoleon who said that an army marches on its stomach. It was Wellington who, probably more than any other military commander during those wars, ensured an efficient supply line. As early as his Indian campaign, he was writing letters about army stores and the transportation of bullocks. His insistence in Mysore that 'if I had rice and bullocks I had men, and if I had men I knew I could beat the enemy' anticipated a chief concern of his in the Peninsula. Wellington's biographer Philip Guedalla offers a vivid metaphor, remarking that 'he waded ankle-deep in questions of supply. He called for beef; he called for sheep; he called for forage.' His despatches frequently requested food for both soldiers and horses, and he regularly pointed out to his government that money was needed for all this. Interestingly, the Peninsular War was significantly funded by the London branch of Rothschild's bank. Anecdotally, James Rothschild of Paris smuggled bullion to Wellington through the French lines disguised as a woman. In August 1809 Wellington wrote to his brother Richard, now envoy to the central Spanish junta, 'A starving army is worse than none. The soldiers lose their discipline and their spirit.' In October 1811, he complained in a letter to Admiral Berkeley: 'I have had enough of sieges with defective artillery and I will never undertake another without the best.' He was acutely aware that even the tiniest detail could make a difference. Hence the boost to morale when in 1813 he arranged for the men's heavy iron kettles to be replaced by light tin cooking pots, and for the infantry to be given tents. This attention to detail was not confined to his troops. Wellington, who described the Peninsula as 'the grave of horses', took what measures he could to reduce his four-footed losses. In the run-up to Talavera, as his army moved from Portugal to Spain, he instructed his officers to make sure the horses got used to eating 'barley or Indian corn or straw', as these were likely to be more plentiful than oats. As Wellington made for Salamanca, he chose to move his army during the summer when the fields by which they marched would be rich in grain for both horses and men. Such considerations were vital, as Masséna had found to his cost during the winter of 1810–11, when his army struggled to survive after Wellington ordered the British and Portuguese to strip the fields bare of crops.

Wellington's concern for the welfare of his men extended to their medical care, which he understood to be as important as good food supplies. He made a point of visiting the wounded in hospital and supported the plans of James McGrigor, his chief medical officer in the Peninsula, to improve their conditions. He was a pioneer of field hospitals as close as possible to the front line to speed up treatment, and although he scolded McGrigor for changing the lines of evacuation of casualties without consulting him, he immediately showed his appreciation of the doctor's work by placing him at his side at the table that evening. He recognised also the imperative of high-quality intelligence, which he tried to gather before the outbreak of hostilities. He made sure that his network of spies, who collected information as to the strength and location of the enemy, were well paid, and made good use of the Spanish resistance in gaining details. In Major-General Sir George Scorell he found a skilful code-breaker, who managed to decipher Napoleon's messages in the build-up to Vitoria. According to Wellington's despatches, at one point in 1813 the War Minister, Lord Bathurst, sent him a box of shoes with false soles 'for conveying written intelligence in an unsuspecting manner'. Accruing intelligence about Napoleon's army strengthened Wellington's hand

29 William Heath (1794–1840)
Punishment Drill, 1830
Etching
Published by Thomas McLean, 1830
National Army Museum, London

when he wrote home for reinforcements. It also enabled him to itemise his battle plans very carefully, leaving nothing to chance and laying great emphasis on timing, which he developed to near perfection.

Crucially, in all this attention to detail, Wellington was a man of discipline, who imposed the high standards he set for himself upon all those he commanded (see plate 29). The Iron Duke indeed claimed that 'There is but one way, – to do as I did – to have A HAND OF IRON.' This principle was set when he found himself in India, with lines of communication 300 miles long, and it was one by which he operated for the rest of his military career. He believed in rigorous preparatory drilling and constant training in battlefield formations, and made sure that his men were always occupied. He wrote to his brother Richard from India: 'A successful army which has nothing to do is very inflammatory' and described them in a despatch to War Minister Castlereagh as 'a rabble', which he was trying to 'tame'. Discipline among soldiers in the Peninsula was, he knew, vital if, in contrast to the French, they were to maintain the goodwill of the local population. To ensure the protection of the Portuguese and their property, he imposed stringent punishments, repeatedly opposing those who wanted to abolish flogging. Neither was he squeamish about hanging soldiers for misconduct. The order was to execute those caught looting from the locals. For him, triumphs at Badajoz and Vitoria were gravely undermined by the looting spree in which his men indulged afterwards and earned for them his tag 'scum of the earth'. He had high standards too for his various chiefs and commanders, for example of artillery and engineering, demanding briefings that were concise and delivered from memory. This was perhaps the last of the old-style wars, in which there was a formal confrontation of two armies in the field. Right to the last, Wellington stuck to the etiquette of such conflict. When, at Waterloo, one of his gunners pointed out, 'There's Bonaparte, Sir; I think I can reach him, may I fire?' Wellington cried, 'No, no. Generals commanding armies have something else to do than to shoot at one another.'

30 Cast of the hands of the Duke of Wellington, *c.*1840
Bronze
Made by Elkington and Company
National Army Museum, London

An autocrat – yes, he might be styled thus. But there is no doubt that his success came partly as a result of the quality of his commanding officers: several of these have had Wellington College houses named after them. As discipline in the ranks improved, he started to place more trust in his officers. One such was Rowland ('Daddy') Hill, loved and respected by his men, whom Wellington first came to know early in his career during the campaign in the Netherlands, and who went with him as a major general to the Peninsula. A contemporary account of Hill fighting soon after their arrival in Portugal declares, 'Few men could have conducted the business with more coolness and quietude of manner, under such a storm of balls as he was exposed to.' Then there was Wellington's friend Lieutenant-General Sir William Beresford, who had been put in charge of the Portuguese army and became, effectively, his second-in-command in the Peninsula. A stubborn character with only one eye, who experienced considerable difficulties in holding the fortress at Badajoz, he proved very effective in turning the Portuguese troops into a disciplined force to fight alongside Wellington. Lieutenant-General Sir Thomas Picton commanded the Third Division (plate 32). A larger-than-life character, whom Wellington described as 'a foul-mouthed devil' while adding 'no man could do better in different services I assigned to him', he had the task of scaling the castle walls at Badajoz using 30-foot ladders. Already seriously wounded, 'If we cannot win the castle', he is said to have cried, 'let's die upon the walls.' Just before midnight, one of Picton's colonels managed to find a vulnerable place in the wall, where he climbed his ladder and mounted the battlements. Thus Picton succeeded in taking the castle. Wellington knew that it was to Picton that he owed his victory at Badajoz. His Third Division was also pivotal at Vitoria, Picton himself leading them forward: 'Come on, ye rascals! Come on, ye fighting villains!' A contemporary account describes how 'Old Picton rode at the head of the third division, dressed in a blue coat and a round hat, and swore as roundly all the way as if he had been wearing two cocked ones.' Picton also distinguished himself in the fighting immediately prior to Waterloo, constantly rallying his men at Quatre Bras as they faced a barrage of charges, losing a horse under him and having two of his ribs broken. He carried on leading the British line forward, telling no one that he had been injured and riding throughout the next day on a borrowed horse without a saddle. As he led his men at Waterloo, Picton was shot through the forehead, but survived.

At Albuera and Badajoz, a bright young staff officer, Henry Hardinge of the Fourth Division, distinguished himself. At Waterloo he represented Wellington at Field Marshal Gebhard Leberecht von Blücher's headquarters and lost a hand in the fighting on 17 June. General Sir Thomas Graham, later Lord Lynedoch, fought with Wellington in the Peninsula, starting off the siege of San Sebastian, the last main Spanish fortress on the way to France. Then there was Lord Uxbridge, Wellington's second-in-command at Waterloo. A contemporary described him as 'a very fine cavalry leader ... with ... dash, activity and resource. But he had too much fire in his temper for cool generalship'. At Quatre Bras

31 Saw and glove used to amputate Lord Uxbridge's leg at Waterloo, 1815
National Army Museum, London

32 Sir Martin Archer Shee (1769–1850)
Lieutenant-General Sir Thomas Picton (1758–1815), c.1830–7
Oil on canvas
Royal Collection, London

he reputedly told his cavalry to 'Make haste! For God's sake gallop, or you will be taken!' Spotting through his telescope the Prussians at last approaching Waterloo, he 'jumped on his horse, and ... dashed off like a whirlwind to meet them'. One of the last shots fired at Waterloo hit Uxbridge in the leg as he sat astride his horse next to Wellington. 'By God, Sir, I've lost my leg.' Wellington glanced down and remarked, 'By God, Sir, so you have.' During the subsequent amputation, Uxbridge's pulse never changed and he later observed to the Marquise d'Assche, 'you see I shan't be able to dance with you any more except with a wooden leg' (see plate 31). Such examples of courage and stoicism indicate the calibre of senior officers with whom Wellington was fortunate enough to work.

The part played by the British infantry in Wellington's success should not be underestimated either. Having notoriously called them 'the scum of the earth', he did later acknowledge, 'It is really wonderful that we should have made them the fine fellows they are.' It was difficult: funds had been poured into the Royal Navy for 50 years, and the British army found itself somewhat neglected. But, under Wellington, it became the force that saved Europe, and he generally gave it credit, writing in a despatch in 1809 to Castlereagh: 'I cannot say too much in favour of the officers and troops.' The thin red line of British infantry became a byword for dogged determination under fire and skilful hand-to-hand fighting. After the siege of Badajoz, Wellington wrote to Prime Minister Lord Liverpool praising 'the gallantry of our troops'. Discussing with civilian Thomas Creevey his imminent confrontation with Napoleon, Wellington pointed to a red-jacketed British infantryman walking nearby in a Brussels park: 'There, it all depends upon that article whether we do the business or not. Give me enough of it, and I am sure.' Undoubtedly the years fighting in the Peninsula had done much to prepare the infantry for Waterloo. Wellington later said that if he had been able to fight at Waterloo with his Peninsula army, he could have beaten Napoleon in three hours, a view shared by rifleman Kincaid, who believed that the 'old Peninsula army ... would have swept his opponents off the face of the earth immediately after their first attack.' But it was still a battle that displayed the British infantry at their best, as they continued to beat off the repeated onslaught of French cavalry attacks. Confessing to his brother Richard that Waterloo was 'the most desperate business I was ever in', Wellington nonetheless declared, 'I never saw the Infantry behave so well.' It was unfortunate that his decision not to single out in his Waterloo despatch any specific regiments or individuals for praise caused some resentment in the ranks. Six years earlier, commenting on Wellington's despatch from Talavera, his brother William had commented, 'you are not warm enough in Praise of your officers ... I think you are particularly cold in praising the Artillery.' For Wellington, perhaps, it was enough for the men to know that they had been partakers in victory. As one who shied away from effusive plaudits, he perhaps failed to grasp that others, less secure in their sense of achievement, required more vociferous praise.

It was not only people who contributed to Wellington's victories. Horses, too, played a significant part in his story. At Angers he learned first-class horsemanship. One of the secrets of his success was therefore his ability to spend hours in the saddle. He would stay at a party until late and then immediately ride a long distance on war business. At Assaye he had to ride three different horses, his first two having been shot under him. Richard Holmes travelled to the scene of this battle and concluded that 'there is particular merit to viewing a battlefield from horseback: that extra few feet of height improves the view'. It was from the back of a horse that Wellington surveyed his battles, directing them from the saddle and relying both on the speed of his horse and on his own skills as a rider. His favourite horse, Copenhagen (whose mother was ridden at the siege of Copenhagen in 1807), was with him for some of his greatest moments (see plate 14): Wellington bought him in Spain and rode him from Vitoria to Waterloo. Like his owner, Copenhagen was brave, energetic and utterly reliable. He had Arab blood and his grandsire was a celebrated racehorse, Eclipse. On his death, Wellington declared, 'There may have been many faster horses, no doubt many handsomer, but for bottom and endurance I never saw his fellow.'

As well as a great horse under him, the Duke had luck on his side. He had many close shaves with death or serious injury, and a number of his comments indicate that he came to believe he led a charmed life. In January 1813 he called himself 'the most fortunate and the most favoured of God's creatures'. After fighting near Pamplona later that year he wrote to his brother William, 'I escaped unhurt as usual, and I begin to believe that the finger of God is upon me.' At the close of Waterloo he exclaimed, 'The hand of almighty God had been upon me this day', writing later to Lady Frances Wedderburn Webster, 'The finger of Providence was upon me, and I escaped unhurt.' In his wife Kitty's opinion her husband was 'protected by a transparent, impenetrable, adamantine Shield ... [so] that he could not be *even touched*; so precious a life.' There is no denying that Wellington had some miraculous escapes – for example, at Talavera, where he was surveying the field from the top of a tower that French sharpshooters almost managed to penetrate. Wellington escaped when he heard their shots, leaping onto his horse and galloping off pursued by French fire. Later in the same battle, a bullet scraped his shoulder and made a hole in his coat. As Peter Snow points out, over the seven years between Wellington's arrival in the Peninsula and the Battle of Waterloo, 'nearly all his close aides were killed or wounded beside him'. At Waterloo, he constantly put himself in danger's way. His aide-de-camp, Fitzroy Somerset, sustained a serious arm injury as he rode by Wellington's side near La Haye-Sainte, while the Duke remained unscathed. At one point, finding himself surrounded by French lancers and hussars, Wellington escaped by leaping over a line of Gordon Highlanders. As he did so, he shouted to them to lower their weapons so that Copenhagen could jump over their heads. After the battle, he had to swerve to avoid being injured by an exhausted Copenhagen, who lashed out when he tried to pat him.

Wellington's luck was not confined to the battlefield. In the early part of his career he was extremely fortunate that his spell in India coincided with his brother Richard's arrival there as Governor-General. Had he not had family in high places, he might have been court-martialled for failing in the attack at Sultanpettah Tope in 1799. Ten years after this incident, early in the Peninsular War, Richard replaced George Canning at the Foreign Office, giving his younger brother smooth access to the seats of power back in London. When Wellington was the Ambassador in Paris, there were a number of attempts on his life, so he was promptly moved to the safety of Vienna, where he acted as British plenipotentiary. He was certainly well looked after.

He was also fortunate in the mistakes made by his enemies. Napoleon's ambitions in Russia diverted French forces away from the Peninsula, and also meant that he did not fight Wellington in person until Waterloo. When that great confrontation came, the emperor was not at his best. On the morning of the battle, he delayed marching until 1pm, to allow the ground to dry after the previous night's downpour. His response when Marshal Ney requested reinforcements was: 'Troops? Where do you expect me to find them? Do you expect me to make them?' This was not someone in control. He gave unclear orders; he changed his orders; he failed to follow up his advantage; he failed to listen to those who had fought Wellington in the Peninsula; he found he was commanding an army that came nowhere near to matching what he was used to fighting with; his own powers had undergone a catastrophic falling off. There is a theory that he was suffering from piles at the time: riding a horse for hours would therefore have been torture. Wellington matched luck with skill and was quick to exploit the enemy's areas of weakness.

Part of the Duke's greatness lay not in his military cunning, nor in his practical attention to detail, not even in the men who fought with him. It lay in his humanity. He was a hero who shed blood because he had to, not because he wanted to. The job had to be done and he carried it

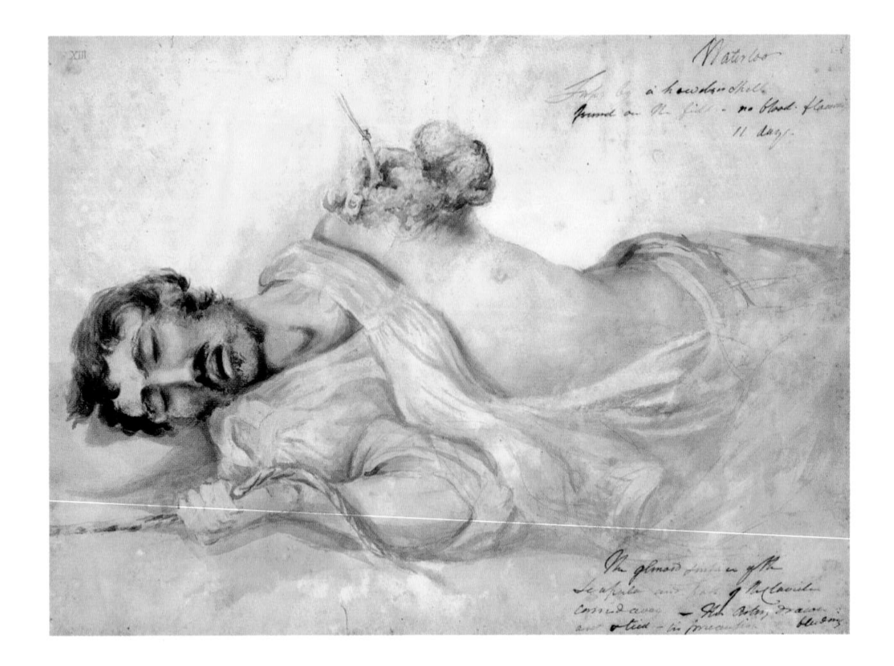

33 Charles Bell (1774–1842)
A British Soldier Wounded at the Battle of Waterloo, 1815
Watercolour
Wellcome Collection

out because that was where his duty lay, but the carnage of war always distressed him. In his despatch after Assaye he wrote: 'I should not like to see again such loss as I sustained ..., even if attained by such gain.' An eyewitness described him sitting motionless that night among the casualties, his head between his knees. He was well aware that war was a messy, uncontainable business. After Talavera, Sir Walter Scott proposed a history of the battle, to which Wellington responded: 'it would be as easy to write the account of a ball as of a Battle! Who was the Partner of Who? Who footed to each other? Who danced down all the couples?' He had no illusions about war being glamorous. A victory that came at considerable cost and that, according to reports, particularly distressed Wellington, was the siege of Badajoz. Dr James McGrigor gave an account of Wellington's appearance as the news of British casualties came through: 'The jaw had fallen, the face was of unusual length, while the torchlight gave to his countenance a lurid aspect.' Similarly, the crayon sketch of Wellington which Goya drew from life that summer shows an exhausted face, haunted eyes staring out (plate 34). When he viewed the battlefield after the Badajoz storming and saw the bodies in the breaches, he broke down in tears. Visiting a nearby hospital, he told the men, 'I am sorry to see so many of you here', to be assured by a sergeant, 'If you had commanded us, my Lord, there wouldn't be so many of us here.' He did what he could to improve the lot of wounded soldiers, changing the rules and so reducing the sum deducted from their pay for hospital treatment. During the Peninsular War, hearing that some wounded men whom he had ordered to be housed in officers' quarters were sleeping out in the open, he rode 30 miles to sort out the matter himself, moving the casualties inside and putting the disobedient officers before a court martial.

Waterloo itself, although a pronounced victory for the allied army, came at a huge cost, with between forty and fifty thousand dead and wounded lying on the battlefield (see plates 23 and 24). Four in every ten of the officers who had attended the Duchess of Richmond's ball had been killed. As Wellington wrote his Waterloo despatch, the body of his friend and aide-de-camp Captain Alexander Gordon was growing cold in his own bed next door, where he had been placed on the Duke's instructions. Wellington was very distressed by the death of Gordon and so many other comrades. Dr Home, Surgeon-General at Waterloo, described how Wellington 'extended his hand to me, which I took and held in mine, whilst I told him of Gordon's death, and related such of the casualties as had come to my knowledge. He was much affected. I felt his tears dropping fast upon my hands.' Wellington then observed to

34 Francisco de Goya (1746–1828)
Arthur Wellesley, 1st Duke of Wellington, Spain 1812
Red chalk drawing over graphite
Stratfield Saye

the doctor, 'I don't know what it is to lose a battle, but certainly nothing can be more painful than to gain one with the loss of so many of one's friends.' Writing to a friend, he confessed, 'My heart is broken by the terrible loss I have sustained of my old friends and companions and my poor soldiers.' To his sister-in-law he insisted, 'Oh, do not congratulate me. I have lost all my dearest friends', and Lady Shelley, with whom Wellington may have had a relationship in Paris after Waterloo, recalls him talking about a condition we would now call post-traumatic stress disorder:

> *It is quite impossible to think of glory. Both mind and feelings are exhausted. I am wretched even at the moment of victory, and I always say that next to a battle lost, the greatest misery is a battle gained ... At such moments every feeling in your breast is deadened.*

Waterloo was Wellington's last battle, as he fervently hoped it would be. For the rest of his life he was particularly generous in giving to orphanages, conscious that he had been an indirect cause of creating many orphans. This is one reason why the founding of Wellington College as his memorial, to educate the orphaned sons of officers, was so appropriate.

Wellington never underestimated the cruelty of war. Neither did he ever underestimate his enemy. Herein lay another of his strengths. Helped by a fluent knowledge of French, he studied Napoleon carefully, telling Gordon that he would 'rather fight fifty thousand men than Bonaparte himself'. His years of fighting the French in the Peninsula put him in a strong position when he came to confront them at Waterloo. Napoleon, by contrast, made the error of despising his opponent. Marshal Soult, who had experienced Wellington's talents at first hand in the Peninsula, must have trembled when the emperor hissed to him as they prepared for Waterloo, 'Just because you have been beaten by Wellington, you think he's a good general. I tell you, Wellington is a bad general, the English are bad troops, and this affair is nothing more than eating breakfast' (see plate 35).

Although Napoleon never studied his opponent's battle tactics, there is evidence that he relied on Wellington's despatches (published in the British press), which were models of lucidity and conciseness, for information rather than on the reports of his generals. His brother William, responding to the despatch from Talavera, commented, 'I have never read so clear or so modest a statement.' Wellington wrote his Waterloo despatch, which ran to just four columns in *The Times*, the morning after the battle, famously describing it as 'the nearest run thing you ever saw in your life'. Contemporary historians continue to be impressed. As Richard Holmes notes: 'To write, largely from memory, a detailed account of the events of 15–18 June, with only a few hours' sleep and so many of his friends killed or wounded, was a prodigious accomplishment.'

Wellington always understood the importance of good communications. His despatches, carefully drafted to keep the government at home informed of his work, were an aspect of his political savviness – a further clue to his overarching success. Early in 1809, Wellington worked hard to support Cabinet members who were in favour of exploiting revolts in Spain and Portugal to undermine Napoleon's position, and asked for additional troops. When his ally Castlereagh stood down as Prime Minister later that year, Wellington wrote to him:

> *I have experienced many acts of friendship and kindness from you. If I had been your brother you could not have been more careful of my interests ... and on every occasion it has always appeared to me that you sought for opportunities to oblige me and to mark your friendship for me.*

Although never on such good terms with Castlereagh's successor, Lord Liverpool, Wellington had been friends with him, and felt free to send back candid reports from the Peninsula. He ensured that the progress of the war there strengthened his position with those in power at home, and was determined to show 'the Croakers' (as he called the politicians who disagreed with him) that he could save Portugal from the French. He always recognised that, alongside his fighting on the field, there were political battles in which he would have to be equally skilful. Sceptics were converted both by his successful storming of Ciudad Rodrigo and subsequent victory at Badajoz, which Wellington used as a platform to

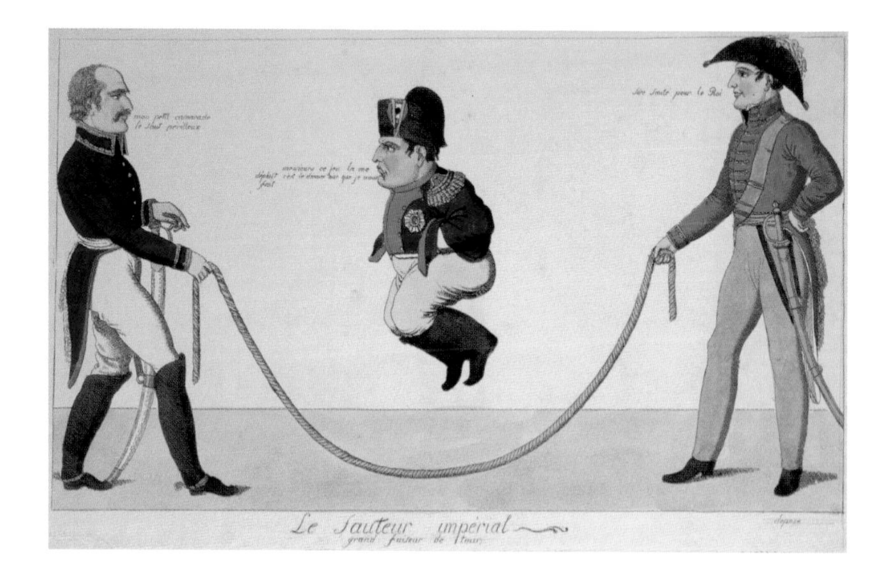

35 Unknown artist
'Le Sauteur Imperial' Bourbon Caricature, July 1815, 1815
Coloured engraving
Private Collection
'The Imperial Jumper'. Blücher (left) and Wellington (right) are in control at either end of the Waterloo skipping rope, forcing Napoleon to exert himself in ways that would have been previously unthinkable. The battle, contrary to the emperor's expectations, proved considerably more demanding than 'eating breakfast'.

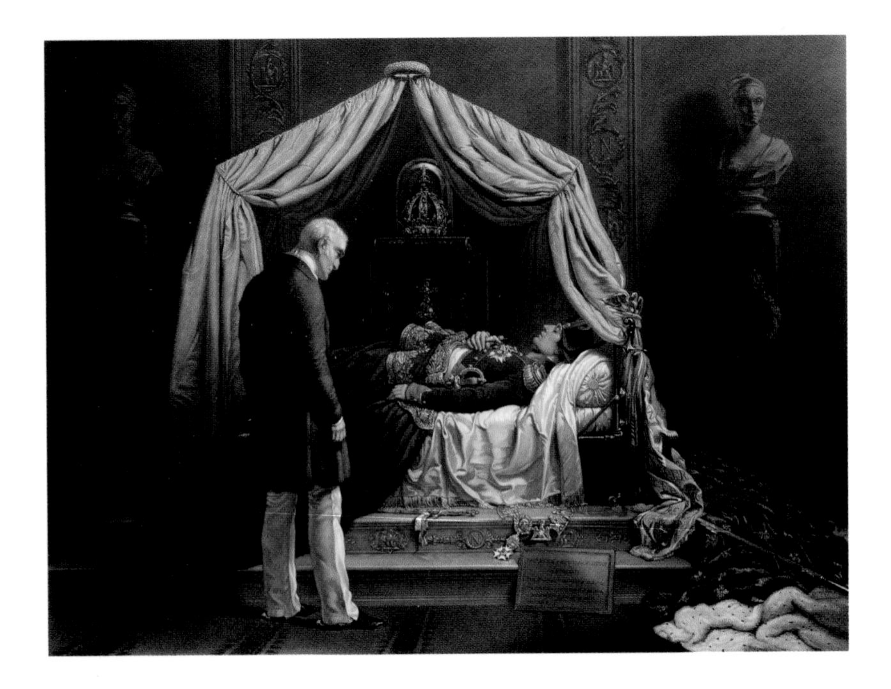

36 James Scott (*c.*1809–*c.*1889) after Sir George Hayter (1792–1871)
The Duke of Wellington Visiting the Effigy and Personal Relics of Napoleon at Madame Tussaud's
Mezzotint
Published 1854
National Portrait Gallery, London

argue with the War Secretary in favour of improved pay for corporals and sergeants. He also exploited the triumphant siege of Badajoz to convince London that a new Corps of Engineers was long overdue.

Wellington understood the importance of being on good terms with the local people during campaigns abroad. This was a particular feature of the Peninsular War, for which Wellington had a strict code of conduct. 'It is almost essential to the success of the army', he declared, 'that the religious prejudices and opinions of the people of the country should be respected.' He forbade all ranks from going to places of religious worship 'during the performance of Divine service' without permission from their superiors, and he insisted that all items supplied by local people should be accounted and paid for. His sensitivity on such matters helped maintain generally good relations with the Portuguese and, later, the Spanish. Certainly the occupying French soldiers fared much worse at the hands of the indigenous population. The British army, by contrast, were greeted joyfully by the city's inhabitants when they marched into Madrid in August 1812, the women making their shawls into a carpet for Wellington's horse to walk on. A few months later he got a hero's welcome in Cadiz and Lisbon, the Spanish resistance leaders inviting him to command their armies. He made a practice of inviting local dignitaries to dine with him and his officers and threw the occasional ball for the locals.

Such diplomacy was most severely put to the test in Wellington's role as an allied commander. In Don Gregorio de la Cuesta, commander of the allied Spanish army, he had to deal with an incompetent general in poor health, who refused to attack the French at Talavera as instructed. 'If he had fought when I wanted him to at Talavera', Wellington claimed, 'I have no hesitation in saying that it would have cleared Spain of the French from that time.' Wellington drew deep into his reserves of tact and tolerance in order to ensure that the British/Spanish alliance was maintained through to the end of the war, and grew to trust them increasingly over time. He seems to have found it more straightforward to work with the Spanish resistance guerrillas, who intercepted French messengers, their secrets then cracked by Wellington's intelligence staff. In Portugal, Wellington managed to incorporate a Portuguese brigade into each of his divisions, extending to them the discipline and practical tactics he instilled in his own men. After the Battle of Bussaco in 1810, in which Portuguese troops fought alongside the British, Portugal felt a new pride in its army.

Wellington's experience of allied combat in the Peninsula served him in good stead at Waterloo, where he was fighting, not just with Field Marshal Gebhard von Blücher's Prussian army, but also with divisions from the Netherlands, Brunswick, Hanover and Nassau. He split his forces under the command of Rowland (Lord) Hill and the Prince of Orange, as well as himself. To reduce vulnerability, he made sure that British and foreign brigades fought alongside each other in their divisions. His triumphant alliance came of course with Blücher, without whom the outcome of Waterloo would have been very different. Napoleon's strategy was to defeat Wellington and Blücher's forces by keeping them separated. Thus the relationship between these two commanders was crucial. After fierce fighting at Ligny, two days before Waterloo, when

37 A.S. Forrest (1869–1963)
Not Till After the Battle Did Blücher and Wellington Meet, 1905
Colour lithograph
Illustration from *Our Island Story* by H.E. Marshall, published by T.C. & E.C. Jack Ltd, London, 1905

Blücher's horse was shot and fell on him, and he only narrowly avoided being trampled on by his own cavalry, many Prussian officers advised him to abandon Wellington. But Blücher stayed firm to the plan they had prepared together and to their overarching resolve to stop Napoleon from reaching Brussels. As Wellington acknowledged in his despatch, 'I should not do justice to my own feelings, or to Marshal Blücher and the Prussian army, if I did not attribute the successful result of this arduous day to the timely assistance I received from them.' He called Blücher's decision to move closer to the allied army on the evening of 17 June, rather than fall back towards Namur or Liege, 'the decisive moment of the century'. Ironically, it was in French that the two men conversed, as neither spoke the other's language. When they met at the appropriately named La Belle Alliance farm at 9pm on 18 June to confirm victory, Blücher cried, 'Mein lieber kamarad, quelle affaire.' Mutual trust and respect, along with a shared determination, had enabled these two 'kamarads' to reach this moment (plate 37).

The Battle of Waterloo was the culmination of all that Wellington had learned and practised over the course of his military career. His key strengths, especially his understanding of topography, his organisation of the troops, his presence on the battlefield and his charismatic leadership, were all spectacularly displayed on 18 June 1815. Even though it has had its detractors among historians, Waterloo remains a profoundly significant battle. Napoleon had tried to take over Europe; Wellington and his allies had stopped him in his tracks. Some have argued that the battle was not won by Wellington but lost by Napoleon, but this distinction is unhelpful. Britain was now the great power of Europe, and as a result of Waterloo the peace terms agreed were more costly for France than they would have been before Napoleon escaped from Elba. More importantly, for 99 years, until the outbreak of the Great War, there was peace in Europe. Near Brussels, whose country's fate was to prompt the outbreak of hostilities on 4 August 1914, and with German allies who almost 100 years later were to be the enemy, Europe's most perilous moment was averted. The importance of Waterloo was recognised by the fact that the Waterloo Medal, awarded to all those who had taken part in the battle, was the first ever to be issued to the entire British army regardless of rank (see plate 47). As a result of the settlement that had been reached at the Congress of Vienna in 1814, monarchies across Europe were restored to power after Waterloo: states were created and some of those that had been dissolved were given to the victors of the Napoleonic Wars; Britain became supremely powerful and dominated world affairs. In Peter Snow's view, the end of the Napoleonic Wars meant that 'the flagrant excesses of the eighteenth-century upper class gradually shifted to the more sober

38 Waterloo Station, *c.*1966

demeanour of the Victorian age. And the man who more than any other embodied that change was Arthur, Duke of Wellington.'

So Waterloo marked the entry into a new European order. Some historians call the period 1815–1914 'Britain's Century': free from French interference, the Pax Britannica was constructed. Historian Andrew Roberts identifies Waterloo as 'the last great eighteenth-century conflict, marked ... by adherence to a certain set of rules of engagement'. This is why Wellington would not allow his artilleryman to fire directly at Napoleon. It has become an iconic battle in the popular consciousness: when someone is said to have 'met their Waterloo', we all understand what is meant. With a twist of dark humour, when Eurostar changed stations from London Waterloo to London St Pancras in 2007, an advertisement in France showed Napoleon surrounded by his soldiers, with the strapline 'Forget Waterloo'. The battle has featured in novels, films and television programmes ranging from *Dad's Army* to *Doctor Who* and *James Bond*. We can only guess at what the Duke would have made of them.

CHAPTER II

Peace, Politics and a Passing

39 Unknown artist
The Duke of Wellington walking in Hyde Park with Mrs Arbuthnot, 1834
Lithograph
Published 1834
Stratfield Saye
The Duke and Mrs Arbuthnot are walking past the Achilles statue as seen on page 68.

So, Waterloo was won, Napoleon would shortly be sent to spend the rest of his truncated life on an island in the middle of the South Atlantic, and the Duke of Wellington was a national – indeed a European – hero. What would be the next phase of this remarkable life? He could not return to England to be lionised in some kind of early retirement. The driving force behind Wellington's career was his desire to serve his country. In the immediate aftermath of June 1815, the best way he could do this was by remaining in Europe and picking up the pieces of more than a dozen years of war. It was perhaps a curious decision of the Prime Minister, Lord Liverpool, to appoint the Duke as the new British Ambassador in Paris; it was certainly not a tactful one. Perspicacious as usual, Wellington found an imposing house ('palace' might be a better word) for the embassy, on the Faubourg Saint-Honoré. The British Ambassador still lives there, conveniently close to the heart of French government at the Elysée Palace and with gardens backing onto the Champs Elysées. Wellington purchased the building from Napoleon's sister Pauline – an interesting footnote to the story.

As Ambassador, Wellington had several pressing tasks: dealing with the new French king, Louis XVIII, a man completely lacking in charisma, who became especially unpopular with his people when it seemed clear that he would be relying on the former enemy, Britain, for help; treading diplomatically over the rift in the French army between royalists and Bonapartists; and pushing the French towards abolition of the slave trade. There were practical things Wellington did that prove the high ethical plane on which he continued to operate in peacetime. For example, he made sure that all the art treasures Napoleon had looted were taken from the Louvre by British and Dutch soldiers. This included

40 The horses of St Mark's Basilica with the Bell Tower in the background, Venice

parts of the Pope's priceless collection, whose return to the Vatican was paid for by the British government. The four horses from St Mark's in Venice, which Napoleon had stolen and erected in the Place du Carousel, were taken down. This was important symbolically also, and was one way in which the Duke answered Madame de Staël's plea to him: 'You must become the greatest man, not of our time, but of all times – and give us back France.' He was expected by all to help France return to normality. Both the aftermath of war and the crisis of a failed harvest in 1816 meant that the country was in dire economic straits. So, in another practical and smoothly-calculated move, Wellington arranged a loan to the French government through Baring Brothers.

Wellington's high profile naturally carried many dangers. There were several attempts on his life during his time in Paris and, later, in Brussels. Just over a year after Waterloo, in late June 1816, he held a ball at the embassy, where a fire was found in the basement, clearly started by gunpowder pushed through the bars from pavement level. The evidence for this failed assassination plot pointed to disgruntled royalists. Another attempt was made in a Brussels park, this time by a Jacobin who referred to Wellington as 'Le Postillon de la Sainte Canaille' – meaning 'Postillion of the Holy Scum', with 'Canaille' being an anagram of 'Alliance'. And so the list continues. A former servant of Wellington's aide-de-camp was offered a bribe by a French ex-officer to assassinate the Duke. Thankfully the man, Ghirardy, refused. Then in January 1818 there were rumours of another plot against Wellington's life. At this point he was in Brussels and preparing to move back to Paris. But he was a very relaxed target and refused to allow the threats to interfere with all he had to do. As he saw it, his key role was to end the occupation of France. This could best be achieved by maintaining national confidence and, in particular, improving France's economic position. He would not be deterred by a rather pathetic collection of vengeful ex-soldiers bent on murdering him.

Matters reached a head in February of that year when one evening, just after midnight, a soldier later identified as André Cantillon shot at Wellington on his way home to the Champs Elysées. Although he was left uninjured, the Paris police investigated this latest assassination attempt, which took them back to the man who had tried to bribe Ghirardy – a grudge-burdened former officer. The British Cabinet called on the Prince Regent to demand that Wellington leave Paris as soon as possible: these unemployed French soldiers were making things too dangerous for him. The Duke's response was typical of the man's courage and his sense of what best guaranteed to keep people calm. In a re-invention of the famous Duchess of Richmond's ball, in which the presence of so many officers, including Wellington himself, prevented panic in Brussels just before Waterloo, he organised a sumptuous ball in Paris at which the guests of honour were the French royal family. As much as in his military career, during this difficult post-war period Wellington knew that sometimes his strongest tactic was to beat a retreat; at other times he needed to stay put. The latter option was the correct one to follow in this instance.

So the Duke of Wellington, victor at Waterloo, our man in Europe, the lynch-pin, it seemed, on which a lasting peace would hang, was what we would now call a celebrity (see plate 41). This can be glimpsed both in the official portraits and in the cartoons, which, incidentally, Wellington loved: this lampooning of himself he found highly entertaining, and was in keeping with his view that the adulation offered one moment by the general public would swiftly change its face the next. But he was keen that the record be kept accurate. One of the famous portraits painted by Sir Thomas Lawrence is a case in point. Lawrence had enormous difficulty painting the sword accurately and Wellington insisted that the artist was forbidden to leave until he had got it right. The fact that 12 years after Waterloo, Wellington could be portrayed in a cartoon as the Greek hero Achilles, albeit 'The Great Captain on the Stool of Repentance', attests to his status as national celebrity (see plate 42). Who, after all, bothers to caricature someone who will not be immediately recognised by all? The context of the cartoon betrays both a reassuringly normal disappointment and rather a large scoop of vanity on Wellington's part: having been passed over by King George IV as

41 A replica of Glasgow's famous Wellington statue being paraded at the 2014 Commonwealth Games

It is a long-standing Glaswegian prank to place a traffic cone on the Duke's head.

42 T. Jones (fl.*c.*1828)
Achilles in the Sulks After His Retreat or, The Great Captain on the Stool of Repentance, 1827
Coloured engraving
Published by G. Humphrey, 7 May 1827
Leeds Art Gallery

43 Sir Richard Westmacott (1775–1856)
Achilles, 1822
Bronze
The Royal Parks, London
Erected in honour of the Duke of Wellington.

Prime Minister in favour of George Canning in April 1827, he refused to serve under Canning and resigned his post as Master-General of the Ordinance and Commander-in-Chief. Outside the Duke's London home on Hyde Park Corner, Apsley House (whose address is the delightfully succinct 'Number 1, London'), a statue of Achilles had been erected in his honour. The cartoon maintained the image of Wellington as the great Greek soldier, but at the point when, early in *The Iliad*, he is sulking in his tent. Wellington was certainly vain when it came to his many portraits, in which he took a great and often critical interest. He even sat for a daguerreotype, so was one of the earliest subjects of what was to become known as photography.

44 Charles Robert Leslie (1794–1859)
The 1st Duke of Wellington Looking at a Bust of Napoleon, 19th century
Oil on canvas
Apsley House, The Wellington Collection, London

Places and objects connected to the famous have always been accorded a special significance – never more so than in the Victorian era. When Victoria was crowned in 1838, two chairs, one for the new monarch and one for the Duke, were created from the elm tree, felled in 1818, which had been Wellington's command post at Waterloo (plate 45). The inscription reads: *To Field Marshal Arthur Duke of Wellington K.G., This Chair, Made of the Elm which on the glorious field of Waterloo witnessed his triumph.* But it was not just the Victorians, of course, who were attached to objects. The Georgians before them had been the first great collectors, and Wellington's celebrity status inspired much souvenir hunting – for example, the famous blue cape he wore at Waterloo that he gave to his friend John Croker, who subsequently lent it to Sir Thomas Lawrence for

45 Thomas Chippendale the Younger (1749–1822)
Waterloo Chair, *c.*1818–20
Royal Collection, London

46 John Constable (1776–1837)
The Opening of Waterloo Bridge ('Whitehall Stairs, June 18th, 1817'), exhibited 1832
Oil on canvas
Tate, London

his portrait of the Duke. Unfortunately, Croker never received the cape back from the artist. Somewhere along the line, a female fan managed to purloin it.

Wellington, in his political life, maintained his supremacy. According to his biographer Richard Holmes, his triumph over Catholic Emancipation 'raised Wellington to an eminence he had not occupied since Waterloo'. Elizabeth Longford comments on the aftermath of the Catholic Emancipation Act in 1829 in *Pillar of State*: 'For a long golden moment national thankfulness flooded all party bounds, giving Wellington a lustre which some thought outshone Waterloo ... Wellington commanded an army of hero-worshippers' (among whom, incidentally, can be found the 13-year-old Charlotte Brontë, who saw in Wellington the great potential 'military King' who would rule over a truly happy nation). But Wellington did not believe in hero-worship and he did not want a history of Waterloo to be written, such literary fanfares being contrary to his taste. Indeed, it is unlikely he viewed with much enthusiasm the 'Waterloo Fair' that flanked the official opening of the new Waterloo Bridge on 18 June 1817 (plate 46). His own private correspondence he destroyed. Doubtless this was primarily to keep secrets safe, but it can also be seen as a gesture typical of someone who disliked pushing his life into the foreground. When, in June 1819, Wellington was given by the state £60,000 in prize money from Waterloo, he immediately returned two-thirds of this to the Treasury. He never forgot that, in the end, it can be the small things that are most valued. Whenever he encountered someone with a medal from the Peninsula or Waterloo (plate 47), he would find a sovereign in his pocket for him. He chose to share the successes of his life with modesty and simplicity.

Of course the other side of the celebrity coin shows the face of resentment, even hatred – especially when unpopular political decisions are being made. It was not just in Paris and Brussels that Wellington's life was put at risk. The Cato Street Conspiracy planned to kill the entire Cabinet at an official dinner after the opening of Parliament on 15 February 1820. Thanks to the conspirators' delays, and also to an effective spy network, the plot was foiled. The Conspiracy's leader, Arthur Thistlewood, had particular hatred for Wellington: 'I had rather kill that D-d villain Wellington than any of them.' In the poet Byron, Wellington found a more articulate foe. Writing in his poem *The Age of Bronze* about the Duke's role at the Congress of Vienna (where the future of Europe was being decided), he railed at 'Proud Wellington, with eagle beak so curled,/That nose, the hook where he suspends the world.'

47 Benedetto Pistrucci (1784–1855)
Waterloo Medal, depicting Wellington, Blücher and the Allied monarchs, 1849
Gutta-percha medal
National Portrait Gallery, London

Eventually the call came, nearly ten years after he first entered the Cabinet. On 9 January 1828, while he was still dressing at Apsley House, Wellington received a note from the Lord Chancellor requesting his presence at Windsor: he was about to become Prime Minister. In a symbolic gesture, Wellington rode to Number 10 Downing Street on Copenhagen – a reminder of his victory at Waterloo. To be a political as opposed to a military leader was, however, never going to be a smooth transition for him. As he remarked to Lady Salisbury: 'I have been accustomed to carry on things in quite a different manner; I assembled my officers and laid down my plan, and it was carried into effect without any more words.' In effect, Wellington was used to operating what many would term a dictatorship. While that is what is needed in wartime, it will not work in peace. Wellington recognised this, and he also understood that the disjuncture between the military world where he had always felt most at home and the political world that was still in many ways alien to him was guaranteed to bring many difficulties. Soon after becoming Prime Minister, he wrote to Colonel Colin Campbell: 'If people think I like this station, they are mistaken. The nation has rewarded me and over-rewarded me. My line is to command the army, but if I think I can do any good by being Minister, I am willing to ... do what I can.'

This meant that, although determined to continue serving his country, Wellington could not always see what it was the country needed. It is perhaps hard to absorb the fact that the hero of Waterloo was, in fact, a reactionary, especially in his opposition to the Reform Bill of 1832, and what many saw as his inadequate response to reform of the Corn Laws. It can also be argued that his sympathy for the idea of Catholic Emancipation was chiefly a function of his background in Ireland. He held 'the mob' in contempt, remaining unmoved by praise as much as by criticism. He was indeed a man who treated the 'two imposters', 'triumph and disaster', both the same. But such an attitude did little to humanise him. The end of the Napoleonic Wars saw times of great hardship in Britain, where industrial depression combined with the plummeting of agricultural prices pushed many to the limit. Victory over France created its own problems: unemployed soldiers now found themselves on the streets. In the post-Waterloo era many of Wellington's compatriots were starving. The population of Britain swelled from 15.74 million in 1801 to 24.15 million 30 years later, and at the same time the proportion dwelling in towns grew considerably. People in the now crowded cities of the Midlands and the North were having to endure great poverty, but remained unrepresented in Parliament. The excessive violence of the French Revolution at the end of the previous century meant that most British people did not favour a radical approach, but they did nonetheless favour political reform. Towards the end of 1818, when Wellington set out on his political career, accepting the post of Master-General of the Ordnance, Britain was suffering from the summer's poor harvest. Its effects were exacerbated by the 1815 Corn Laws fixing prices. The state of the nation was not something that Wellington, in his new incarnation, seemed well fitted to fight. Even General Alava, Wellington's Spanish ally, declared that, 'The Duke of Wellington ought never to have had anything to do with politics.' Indeed, in the view of his biographer Philip Guedalla, 'His subsequent career in politics has done more, perhaps, than any other influence to efface his memory ... The Duke became a stiff-necked conqueror trailing an unwelcome scabbard into civilian assemblies.' C.M. Crutwell, writing in the 1930s, described him as 'the worst Prime Minister of the nineteenth century'. W.H. Maxwell attributes Wellington's unpopularity during his time in politics to the fact that 'he went against the wishes of the people on the great question of reform, and he was not always happy in giving expression to his opinions.' Wellington was quite open about his determination to resist reform, but at a time of hardship and unrest, it was reform that was needed. Wellington, a Tory to the core, failed to understand that this was not the time to do battle with those opposing the status quo.

Wellington's miscalculation as to which way the nation was moving is best shown in the event whose name grimly echoes the moment of his greatest victory. In just ten minutes, on 16 August 1819 at St Peter's Field,

48 Unknown artist
Peterloo Massacre, Manchester, 16 August 1819, c.1819
Wood engraving

Manchester, a one-sided battle was fought. It is now known as Peterloo. Around 80,000 men, women and children had come together to hear Henry 'Orator' Hunt address a meeting of workers from the Lancashire cotton industry. He was calling for reform. Contrary to a ruling from Cabinet, panic-stricken local magistrates read the Riot Act. Unable to disperse the peaceful, unarmed crowd, soldiers on horseback from the yeomanry, joined by the 15th Hussars, cut off all means of escape from the field, which soon began to pile up with trampled bodies. Ten minutes later, as Longford expresses it, 'a light breeze lifted the dust-cloud to reveal something ominously like the aftermath of Waterloo, except that among the torn caps, hats, shoes, ripped-up banners and broken shafts was a wreckage of shawls, bonnets and children's clothes.' Eleven people died; nearly five hundred were wounded.

What is particularly chilling is Wellington's response to the tragedy. Along with 13 other ministers, he signed a letter formally expressing approval of the magistrates' decisions – with the exception of their chairman's reading of the Riot Act. 'It is very clear to me', he remarked, 'that they won't be quiet till a large number of them "bite the dust" ... or till some of their leaders are hanged, which would be the most fortunate result.' His concern that the magistrates, as the representatives of law and order, should feel well supported by government is a concept that would have been readily understood by many nearly two hundred years ago, but seems, to the modern mind, to be missing the point. That Wellington despised 'the mob' is widely and uncomfortably evident. To Lady Shelley he wrote: 'The mob are too contemptible to be thought about for a moment.' This was well illustrated when, after the vote on the repeal of the Corn Laws, workmen cheered the Duke as he left the House of Lords. His response to this show of support was, 'For Heaven's sake, people, let me get onto my horse.' Not surprisingly, he held a poor opinion of journalists: 'for my part, I will have no communication with any of them.'

Neither were the upper classes spared the disapproval of the Iron Duke. He believed they were at fault for some of the nation's ills, travelling abroad rather than staying at home and providing much-needed employment. As we shall see later, he had no illusions either about the nature of the royal family he served. But he was at heart an aristocrat as well as a Tory, sprung from the Anglo-Irish elite. What he saw of democracy he disliked, especially when it bore on its current the sad, sordid and humiliating farce of George IV's divorce from Queen Caroline. Against a life dedicated to politics there were more personal warnings. Wellington's old friend, the Foreign Secretary Lord Castlereagh, committed suicide in 1822. Witnessing at first hand the agonising death on the tracks of MP William Huskisson as he viewed the new Liverpool–Manchester railway will have highlighted for Wellington the perils of public duty. It certainly put him off railways for life.

If, according to Shelley, Castlereagh wore a 'mask', so did Wellington, described by Longford as one of iron. But he understood that this image was needed in order for him to complete what needed to be done – and he certainly had his successes. One of these was his suggestion, finally realised during his premiership in 1829, that Home Secretary Robert Peel should establish a police force. Wellington was insistent that the police should be clearly distinct from the military. So the Iron Duke, having led a great army to victory in wartime, was responsible during peacetime for what has evolved into our modern police force. It specifically confronted crime in the capital, crucially from one central base. It was from its very foundation that London's police force operated from Scotland Yard. We cannot simply relegate the man's views on maintaining law and order to the annals of the Peterloo catastrophe: Wellington did at least recognise that the move from a military to a civilian force provided a reasonable solution. This was the man, after all, who was rigorous in maintaining a disciplined army (right up to the end of his life he opposed all attempts to end corporal punishment in the military), and who would doubtless have attributed much of his wartime success to this discipline. For Wellington, to be 'controlled by the strong arm of authority and law' was integral to the nation's well-being, whether the opponent was a power-hungry French conqueror or the spectres of starvation and riot.

Another of Wellington's achievements came in the Catholic Emancipation Act of 1829. His upbringing made him well suited to understanding the problems faced by Irish Catholics. He warned George IV that rebellion in Ireland was likely and saw Catholic Emancipation as the best way of avoiding this. In 1821 he refused an invitation to join the Orange Order. He always distrusted political societies, whether Protestant or Catholic, radical or defensive. Four years later he drafted a plan for peace in Ireland. At the forefront of this lay his belief that the Union should be maintained, but relief granted to Catholics. His opening of the second reading of the Emancipation Bill in the Lords at the end of March 1829 was delivered without notes and with confident authority. He had seen enough war in his lifetime, he said, and specifically enough civil war, to take all measures necessary to avoid the conflict he believed was imminent in Ireland. He stood fast by his determination to sort out at least some of that country's deep-seated difficulties, even when it meant alienating fellow Tories.

A further issue with which Wellington had to contend was the reform of the Corn Laws. In principle, he supported the Corn Bill, which would reduce the duties payable on corn and so lower food prices at a time of great poverty. What he aimed for, however, was a solution that would give restless town dwellers just a grain of satisfaction: by instinct, he was on the side of the land and of agricultural profit. In his opinion, a drastic reduction in the price of corn would be disastrous for poor farm workers. During the heated negotiation surrounding the Corn Bill, Wellington was under the misapprehension that his compromise solution had been accepted: as a result the Bill's passage through Parliament was rough. The blame for this was directed at Wellington. The revised law fixed the price to which English corn had to rise before foreign corn was imported and then sold virtually duty free. Although the passing of the Bill was followed by four years of poor harvests, with people also gambling on prices, the fact that it became law shows that Wellington's iron did perhaps contain a flexible element.

The next hurdle was the Reform Bill – one in which Wellington did not cover himself in glory. The growth in urban populations, with no matching increase in electoral constituencies in these areas, meant that huge numbers of people did not have a Member of Parliament. Meanwhile the so-called 'rotten boroughs', totally unrepresentative, returned MPs from constituencies where no one, or virtually no one, lived – let alone voted. The issue leading to the Reform Bill was Peel's determination to remove rotten boroughs in Cornwall and Nottinghamshire from representation in the Commons. Instead, many of the urban middle class would have a vote. This was an idea that found no favour with Wellington and a compromise solution worked out in Cabinet was defeated by the House of Lords. Speaking in Parliament in response to the reform proposals put

49 James William Muller (1812–1845)
Queen's Square during the Bristol Riots, 30th October 1831, 1831
Watercolour on paper
Private Collection

forward by Opposition Leader Lord Grey, he declared that he was 'not prepared to bring forward any measure of this nature'. Then he quietly addressed his Foreign Secretary Lord Aberdeen: 'I have not said too much, have I?' But he had, and his intransigent speech showed people all too clearly that he was simply unable to move with the times. There were even threats on his life.

Soon afterwards, in mid-November 1830, Wellington's government was defeated in the Commons on a relatively minor issue, but it was the excuse many felt they needed. That evening Wellington was visited at Apsley House by three ministers, including Peel, who informed him that he must go. The next day, he resigned. The stepping down of the Prime Minister meant that Parliament had to be dissolved. Meanwhile Apsley House was attacked by rioters, who neither knew nor cared that the Duchess of Wellington lay dying inside. Doubtless the Duke would have said this justified his opinion of the mob, and they had not finished with him either. When the following year, in October 1831, Wellington led the Lords against the new Reform Bill, his windows were smashed again. One could argue, however, this was a minor assault compared to what occurred in Bristol, where rioters also protested over the relentless opposition to the Bill. Hundreds of people died when troops intervened and half the city centre was burnt down (see plate 49).

Politics proceeded on its relentless path. Lord John Russell's Third Reform Bill was flung out thanks to a vote in the Lords in the middle of April 1832. So now it was time for Lord Grey to resign and Wellington found himself having to form another Tory government. By mid-May he realised he could not find enough people willing to serve. This cleared the way for King William IV to ask Grey to return as Prime Minister; the Reform Bill became law on 7 June 1832. Although it is known as the 'Great' Reform Act, its scope was in fact very modest (plate 50). Well-populated towns were still, in all too many cases, severely under-represented in Parliament when compared to places of low population density. For Wellington, public dismay at his opposition to the Bill was something that even the memory of Waterloo could not neutralise. On 18 June 1832 he was threatened by a mob that followed him all the way from the Royal Mint to Apsley House. Since the earlier attack on his home, Wellington now protected its windows with iron shutters. Perhaps for the first time in his life he allowed himself to be affected by the people's opinion of him. When asked to step down as Prime Minister, he declared that he was only too ready to go, having 'never had a dispute or a difference with anybody' until he took on that office. He simply seemed unable to distinguish between reform and radicalism. Twice he had to resign as Prime Minister, for the country was moving on and he was not moving with it.

50 Sir George Hayter (1792–1871)
The House of Commons, 1833–43
Oil on canvas
National Portrait Gallery, London
This painting commemorates the passing of the Great Reform Act in 1832 and depicts the first session of the new House of Commons on 5 February 1833. It features some 375 figures including the Duke of Wellington at the bottom right, wearing a red cravat and conferring with colleagues.

It is tempting at this point to cast a glance at that other great wartime leader turned Prime Minister, Winston Churchill, if only to consider the extent to which military strategy might offer a useful background to the machinations of political life. Some will argue that, in the case of both Wellington and his twentieth-century equivalent, their tactics proved much stronger on the battlefield than in peacetime. One supreme skill of Churchill's that the Duke lacked was charismatic public speaking. As a result of the years spent on active service abroad, Wellington lost all his back teeth. His parliamentary speeches were therefore difficult to hear. In 1822 his hearing had been damaged by an explosion during a review of guns he attended as Master-General of the Ordnance. He subsequently endured a great deal of pain and a form of tinnitus. Treatment by an ignorant doctor who applied a strong caustic solution only made matters worse. Wellington permanently lost all hearing in his left ear and for the rest of his life suffered from recurring bad health – which, of course, he always did his best to overcome, it being quite contrary to his nature to take a rest.

Wellington certainly possessed the decisiveness and, if needed, ruthlessness required in political life. This applied not only to his enemies, but also to those in his own party. When, for example, William Huskisson offered his resignation over difficulties in passing through Parliament the Cabinet's plans for rotten boroughs, Wellington accepted his colleague's resignation – and stuck to it. So when Huskisson went on to claim that his resignation had been a mistake, Wellington insisted, 'There is no mistake, there can be no mistake, there shall be no mistake.' Then he went off for a stroll in Birdcage Walk so that he would be out if Huskisson called. His attitude to loyalty and consistency in the party was not dissimilar to what he had expected of his fellow officers in the army, demanding 'What is the meaning of a party if they don't follow their leaders? Damn 'em! Let 'em go!' As we have already seen, he admitted that disagreement, discussion and debate were not concepts with which he had grown familiar in his army years. But the strategic planning that had been such a key foundation of Wellington's military success was certainly something that could be later transferred to cunning and delicate negotiations. As Richard Holmes puts it: 'Wellington took almost as much trouble marshalling his troops for Catholic Emancipation as he had over preparing the lines of Torres Vedras.' Despite this, he was often impatient of the care that needed to be taken in soothing people's petty anxieties and injured pride. When he first became Prime Minister he complained to John Croker, as he pointed at his red boxes, 'There, there is the business of the country, which I have not time to look at – all my time being employed in assuaging what gentlemen call their *feelings*.'

51 Unknown artist
King George IV (1762–1830), c.1820
Engraving
Underneath is an inset of Napoleon Bonaparte (1769–1821) in exile on the island of St Helena.

It was Wellington's dealings with George IV that he himself most explicitly likened to a battle, fought out a few inches at a time. His relationship with the monarchy is pertinent here, given that Wellington College was a 'royal and religious foundation', in which Queen Victoria and Prince Albert took a lead and continued to take a keen interest. The Duke's views on British royalty were most severely tested when George IV was on the throne: he complained that 'he speaks and swears so like an old Falstaff, that damn me if I am not ashamed to walk into a room with him.' To his close friend and diarist Harriet Arbuthnot he described the king as the worst man he had encountered in his life, 'the most false, the most ill-natured, the most entirely without one redeeming quality'. As Lord High Constable of England, Wellington, along with his two sons, wore outfits at the king's coronation costing £1,000. In contrast, Kitty, characteristically, opted for cornelians rather than diamonds, given the poverty in which so many people were living at the start of the reign.

Wellington realised, of course, that whatever his private opinion of the king, it was just part and parcel of serving his country that he would

Napoleon at St Helena.

have to try and put up with him. An episode that tested him to the limit was George IV's stormy marriage to Queen Caroline of Brunswick. Negotiations between the pair, in which Wellington represented the government, came to nothing. The 'Pains and Penalties' Bill threatened to remove the Queen's title and dissolve the marriage. As the government's go-between, Wellington was perceived as a chief player in Caroline's suffering. Her trial in the House of Lords in August 1820 provided another occasion on which Wellington was attacked by the mob, which tried to drag him from his horse.

Wellington needed to use all his tact and skill in persuading George IV to assist the progress of the Catholic Emancipation Bill, which of course required the royal assent. He identified the king's role as to negotiate with his deeply anti-Catholic brother, the Duke of Cumberland. When Wellington threatened to resign if the Bill crashed, the king, breaking down in tears, agreed to support him. The exasperation Wellington felt in his dealings with the man can be most tellingly explained by the fact that, the following day, George IV changed his mind. Thus Wellington embarked on a series of manoeuvres that eventually won him his battle: rather than lose his government, the king capitulated. Even after he died

52 Sir George Hayter (1792–1871)
The Trial of Queen Caroline, 1820–23
Oil on canvas
National Portrait Gallery, London

in June 1830, George continued to haunt his Prime Minister, who had to arrange for an annuity of £6,000 to be paid to Mrs Maria Fitzherbert, whom the late king had secretly and illegally married. This might best be described as 'hush money'. He also had all her papers burned in 1833. Looking at George's corpse, the sharp-eyed Wellington noticed Mrs Fitzherbert's miniature in a locket under his nightshirt.

The Duke of Cumberland continued to be a thorn in Wellington's side. He had, so the gossip ran, committed incest with his sister Princess Sophia and fathered a son by her. Wellington ensured that all paper trails were burned. (In the event, the son – Thomas Garth – turned out to have a different father.) Wellington was a man of such integrity, who understood to his core that the wayward royals had to be endured and protected for the sake of national stability. It would never have occurred to him to use incriminating evidence against Cumberland, the man who proclaimed himself the sworn enemy of Catholic Emancipation.

The Duke's relations with the young Queen Victoria were happily more cordial. He may not have adored her in the way that Churchill did the 25-year old Princess Elizabeth, but for her part Victoria was eager to venerate her experienced Prime Minister, who had secured the greatness of her country. Three years after her coronation, in August 1840, Wellington sat next to her at a banquet and they enjoyed indulging in some glasses of wine together. Wellington remarked of the new monarch: 'She not merely filled her chair; she filled the room.' When Lord Melbourne asked Victoria if she had a preference for anyone, she responded immediately, 'There is but one person ... and that is the Duke of Wellington.' There were occasions when the Duke fell out of favour with the young Queen (he was, after all, a Tory, and she supported the Whigs), and she even threatened not to invite him to her wedding. But he was there, of course, and as she and Albert drove back to Buckingham Palace after their ceremony on 10 February 1840, the only cheer from the public that was louder than theirs was for the elderly Duke. When the Prince of Wales was christened in 1842 Wellington carried the Sword of State, and he was godfather to Prince Arthur, named for him. On hearing of his death in 1852, Victoria described the Duke as 'the most *devoted* and *loyal* subject, and the staunchest supporter the Crown ever had.'

Victoria stayed at Wellington's home at Stratfield Saye and sought his advice on problems of all kinds, including what to do about the sparrows that had taken over the glasshouse set up for the Great Exhibition of 1851. 'Try sparrow-hawks, Ma'am', was the Duke's response. He respected Prince Albert, whom he said should succeed him at Horse Guards – although not just yet, as he was a mere 81, with plenty of years to go. When Wellington died, Albert commented that it was 'as if in a tissue a particular thread which is worked into every pattern was suddenly withdrawn.' To his brother Ernst, he wrote, 'The whole world has suffered a loss. We especially have lost a good friend.' It is sobering to think that the young prince outlived the old soldier by only nine years.

Wellington doubtless enjoyed the young queen's company. In fact, he relished spending time with many women who were not his wife. Elizabeth Longford points out that, given the high numbers, it is likely that these relationships were of an innocent nature. Wellington was observed flirting with Lady Frances, wife of Captain James Wedderburn Webster, at the Duchess of Richmond's ball. She was just 22 at the time and seven months pregnant. He wrote her a message from his tent on the eve of Waterloo. On 5 August 1815 the *St James's Chronicle* offered a shot across the bows, telling its readers that Captain Wedderburn Webster was seeking damages from Wellington. According to the paper, the latter had agreed to pay up. It later transpired that, far from bringing an action for adultery, the Captain, his wife joining him in the move, was suing the *St James's Chronicle* for libel. In February 1816 the court reached a verdict fining the paper £2,000 – a huge sum of money in those days. Yet again, Wellington and his circle were discovering the perils of celebrity.

The woman to whom Wellington was closest in his life – closer, arguably, than he was to poor Kitty, although it was definitely a matter of friendship and not an affair – was Mrs Harriet Arbuthnot (see plate 39). Unlike his wife, Harriet loved talking politics. Wellington found that he came to depend on her presence, her conversation and her letters. The nickname he gave her, 'La Tyranna', came from her insistence on organising his social calendar. In a letter written to Harriet on 13 September 1822, just before he left England, he put in a touching request: 'I hope you will think of me sometimes, and wherever I may be, you may feel certain that my thoughts and wishes are centred on you, and my desire that every action of my life may please you. God bless you. Your most devoted and affection Slave.' In August 1832, hearing that Harriet was dead, Wellington gave himself up to his grief. His friendships with women continued, but Harriet could never be replaced.

Although the Duke was not sentimental about places, he was always very fond of Stratfield Saye, the home in Hampshire bought for him by the nation in 1817 as a gesture of gratitude (see plate 54). It remains the country residence of the Wellington family to this day, just as Apsley House on Hyde Park Corner remains its London home. Stratfield Saye's £263,000 price tag was typical of the Duke's desire for minimum fuss, being less than half the sum granted by Parliament for the purpose. 'Stratfield Saye survives as one of the most pleasant stately homes of England', in Richard Holmes's opinion, 'dignified without being grand,

53 John Hayter (1800–1895)
Portrait of Catherine, 1st Duchess of Wellington, 1828
Stratfield Saye

and accessible in a way that Blenheim Palace, built to celebrate the victories of the Duke of Marlborough, is not.' It was originally built in 1630 by William Pitt, ancestor of his more famous namesakes.

It was Wellington's wife Kitty who particularly loved their Hampshire home. So, for her sake, Wellington abandoned his plans to aggrandise it. Peel considered the house 'wretched ..., wretchedly furnished, but warm and not uncomfortable. The drawing room very small and low, but a handsome library built, I suppose, by the Duke, with a billiard room only separated by columns from the library.' Wellington made the old riding school into a real tennis court. Somewhere in the grounds of Stratfield Saye the faithful Copenhagen lies buried, but when he was asked by the

54 Stratfield Saye House, 2014
Home of the Dukes of Wellington since 1817.

United Services Museum if he would be willing to donate the horse's skeleton, to go alongside that of Napoleon's Marengo, the Duke had no idea where exactly the precious bones lay.

Stratfield Saye also provided an opportunity for Wellington to offer to others the service that was so integral to his values. A generous landlord, he would reduce the rent if a tenant was struggling to pay. He encouraged his steward in the relief of the poor – for example, distributing coal to his tenants so that they did not feel compelled to burn their fences when they needed fuel. Another instance of the Duke's concern for people's welfare is shown in his treatment of the Duke of Alava, from the Peninsula years, forced in 1823 to flee from Spain. Wellington welcomed his old friend to the Stratfield Saye estate, providing him with a house and telling him that as long as he had any money in his account with Coutts Bank, Alava should feel free to draw on it.

Family life at Stratfield Saye did not always present a happy picture. Wellington's marriage to Kitty, conducted in haste after a long interval during which they had not seen each other, provided neither of them with the deep companionship they must have craved. One of the reasons Wellington sought the company of lively, attractive, intelligent women was that he could not find these qualities in his wife. His ex-aide-de-camp, Lord William Lennox, described Kitty as 'amiable, unaffected and simple-minded'. Sophisticated she was not. Nor was she a dazzling society hostess or a particularly competent manager of the household finances (see plate 55). Kitty was more interested in keeping the servants cheerful and distributing money to the poor than in entertaining important people and keeping abreast of paperwork. She must have spent many unhappy hours over the course of the marriage lamenting the fact that she could not be the sort of wife the great Duke expected her to be. It is possible that she may sometimes have misinterpreted his rather peremptory manner of speaking, not understanding that he found it hard to distinguish between making a suggestion to his wife and barking out a military order. She also never fully recognised that, for her husband, home was as much the army mess as a pleasant house in Hampshire.

Wellington believed he treated her well, claiming to Harriet Arbuthnot that he never said a harsh word to her in his life. He also told this confidante that he had made huge efforts to create an amicable relationship with her, but that – the cry of husbands over the centuries – she did not understand him. In Harriet's not impartial opinion, Kitty was 'totally unfit for her situation. She ... dresses herself exactly like a shepherdess, with an old hat made by herself stuck on the back of her head, and a dirty basket under her arm.' When Kitty asked her husband for an increase in her personal allowance, he refused point blank, presumably because

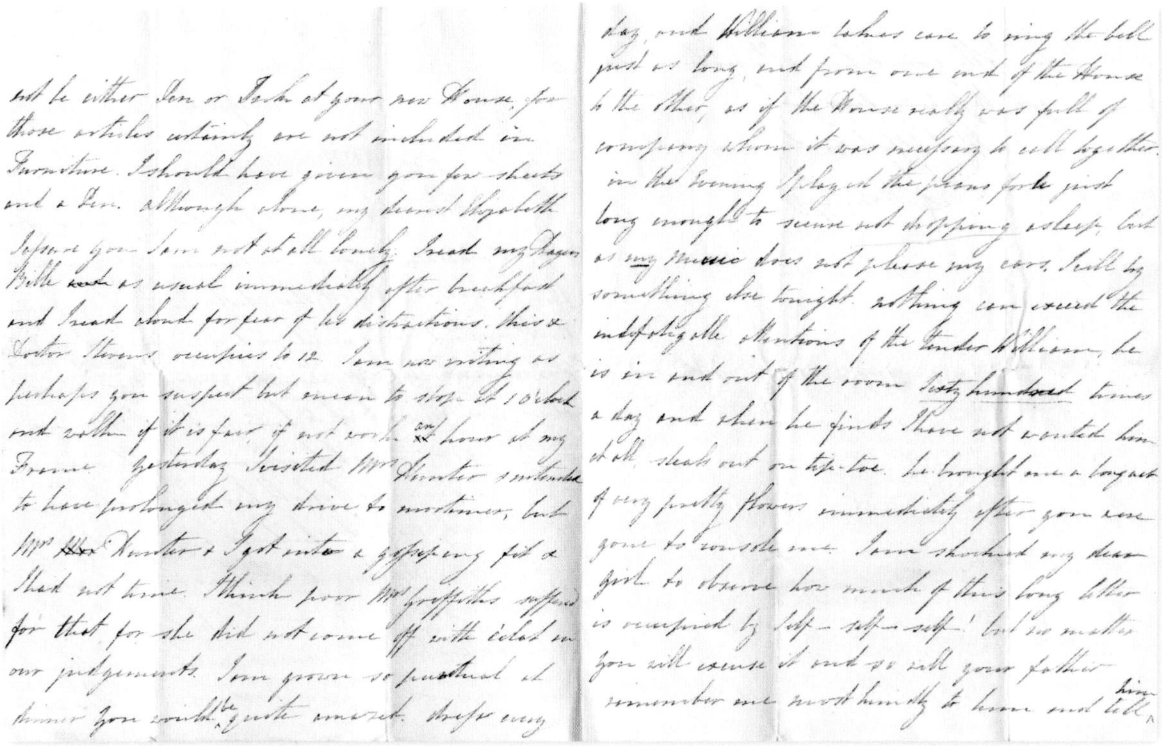
not be either Ten or Tosh at your new House, for those articles certainly are not included in Furniture. I should have given you for sheets and a Ten. Although alone, my dearest Elizabeth I assure you I am not at all lonely. I read my Prayer Bible as usual immediately after breakfast and I read aloud for fear of distractions. this & Doctor Stevens occupies to 12. I am now writing as perhaps you suspect but mean to stop at 1 o'clock and walk if it is fair if not work an hour at my Frame. Yesterday I visited Mrs Hunter & intended to have prolonged my drive to Mortimer, but Mrs Hunter & I got into a gossiping fit & I had not time. I think poor Mrs Griffiths suffered for that for she did not come off with eclat in our judgements. I am grown so punctual at dinner you would be quite amazed. Prayers every

day, and William takes care to ring the bell just as long, and from one end of the House to the other, as if the House really was full of company whom it was necessary to call together. In the Evening I played the piano forte just long enough to secure not dropping asleep, but as my music does not please my ears, I will try something else tonight. Nothing can exceed the indefatigable attentions of the tender William, he is in and out of the room sixty hundred times a day and when he finds I have not wanted him at all, steals out on tip-toe. he brought me a bouquet of very pretty flowers immediately after you were gone to console me. I am shocked my dear girl to observe how much of this long letter is occupied by self – self – self! but no matter you will excuse it and so will your father remember me most kindly to him and tell him

55 Letter from the 1st Duchess of Wellington to Miss Elizabeth Hume, 22 January 1824

The Duchess stuck doggedly to her strengths, preferring to write letters to the family – of whom she was very fond – to keeping notes on the household accounts, which terrified her.

he knew the bulk of this would be spent on her numerous good causes and not on making herself look like the Duchess she should be. She made concessions: at his request, she eventually covered her hair with a wig when she started to turn grey. But she never managed to develop any dress sense (even her son Douro advised his mother that her clothes were 'inconsistent with your station in the world'); she was short-sighted; she was shy.

Kitty was, however, a devoted mother to Arthur and Charles, although her unsatisfactory relationship with her husband made for difficulties in the family dynamic. Wellington's older son, Douro (plate 56), claimed that his father had 'never even patted me on the shoulder when I was a boy, but it was because he hated my mother'. It was not until the boys were grown up that they fully realised how unhappy their parents' marriage had been: both mother and father were successful in hiding this from them. It is probably fair to say that they wanted what was best for the boys, and Arbuthnot's claims that the Duchess pitted them against their father missed the point about her essential loyalty. Kitty arguably had some success in protecting her two sons from the high expectations placed on them by their father. As he contemplated a bust of his father, she heard young Douro sigh, 'My nose is *such a time a-growing*.'

56 Ethel Mortlock
(1878–1928)
Arthur Richard Wellesley, 2nd Duke of Wellington, Lord Lieutenant of Middlesex, c.1903
Oil on canvas
Middlesex Guildhall Art Collection

He continued to speculate: 'Think what it will be like when the Duke of Wellington is announced and only I come in.' His was the hardest of inheritances. Their father, determined that they should improve their minds, set the boys reading lists, tasks in recitation and Latin themes. His corrections were devoid of praise. He also offered advice on their choice of companions:

> *Of all the evils that surround a person in your situation, bad company is the most fatal ... In all stations there are persons of good and bad Education, manners and habits; I earnestly entreat you to associate with the former alone and to avoid the latter, be they or what Rank or Station they may.*

It is worth noting that, for Wellington, it was qualities of character that were crucial to a person's value, and the College that bears his name continues to develop this concept.

Douro was greatly impressed by this letter of his father's, telling Kitty in June 1823:

> *I intend to keep my copy of it as a memorial of the wisest and best of fathers that ever mortal had; I had once thought him the most intense disciplinarian that ever lived, and consequently avoided and feared him accordingly. Lately I have found out what he really is, ... the greatest man that ever lived.*

This is still, of course, something of a burden for any son to carry.

While elder son Douro agonised, his younger brother Charles was, predictably, more light-hearted and outgoing by nature. In 1825, Charles was rusticated for a year from Oxford for painting red all the dons' doors at his college (Christ Church) and then breaking out of college after a dinner party in Douro's rooms. Their father, more furious, it seemed, with the university authorities than with his sons, moved both young men to Trinity College, Cambridge. Not surprisingly, Christ Church objected strongly when Wellington was proposed as Chancellor of Oxford in 1834. As a postscript to the story of Wellington's relationship with his sons, it is worth noting that he derived enormous pleasure from their company, and that of their wives, in his old age, as well as being a devoted grandfather to Charles's children.

Kitty died in 1831, at Apsley House, as the Reform Bill came into being. The cause of death is not certain, but it may have been cancer or cholera. Wellington retreated from a political world whose new directions he did not fully understand and stayed at his wife's bedside. They held hands and she ran a finger up his sleeve to trace the outline of an amulet she once gave him, and which she now discovered he still wore.

57 Joseph Mallord William Turner (1775–1851)
The Burning of the Houses of Parliament, c.1834–35
Watercolour and gouache on paper
Tate, London

As they came closer in her death than they had been in so many years, he thought to himself how strange it was that people could live together for half a lifetime and only understand one another at the end. Kitty's death on 24 April came two days after the king dissolved Parliament. She was buried in the family vault at Stratfield Saye and her husband went on to survive her by 21 years.

When you are the Duke of Wellington and the nation looks to you as to a beacon shining back on a glorious past and forward to try and make sense of the future, you can never simply be a family man. It was in the autumn of 1834 that the Houses of Parliament burnt down, in a conflagration vividly recorded by Joseph Mallord William Turner, and leading William IV to request that Wellington form a caretaker government (see plate 57). This may be seen as a metaphor of uncertainty persisting at the helm, a sense of the vulnerability of the places where power is seated, and a reminder, 19 years after Waterloo, of how swiftly the merely physical may be destroyed. For Britain, it was as if Wellington seemed to represent something that might, after all, last beyond most. First and foremost, Wellington saw himself as there to serve his country, partly in his political work: 'He must be a servant of the country first, of party second' as he wrote to the Prime Minister Lord Liverpool back in 1818, and 'please God however I may suffer I shall succeed in establishing in the Country a strong Government', his words to Harriet Arbuthnot ten years later. But it was not just a matter of politics: he served the needs of his country also in a range of other areas, from dealing with agricultural workers' grievances to improving the Tower of London, working for the Society for the Promotion of Christian Knowledge and helping Ireland confront the threats of potato famine, poverty and absentee landlords. His favourite school of painting was the Dutch (see plate 58): he loved order, and for the light of things as they truly are to be shining on the perceived world.

Part of this notion of service to one's country came through education. The Duke became a governor of Charterhouse School in 1830, insisting that he would give help only to the families of his veterans, and only to those in need. Four years later he accepted the role of Chancellor of Oxford University: 'I am the Duke of Wellington and, *bon gré mal*

58 Peeter Gysels (1621–1690)
A Flemish Village: The River Landing Stage, c.1650–c.1680
Oil on copper
Apsley House, The Wellington Collection, London

59 William Barnes Wollen (1857–1936)
Duke of Wellington's Duel with George Finch-Hatton, 10th Earl of Winchilsea, Battersea Fields, on 21 March 1829, c.1920
From *Cassell's History of England*, published by Cassell and Company Limited
Private Collection

gré must do as the Duke of Wellington does.' He was amused to see, at a Buckingham Palace banquet in July 1837, his own place card simply describing him as 'Chancellor of Oxford', nothing else. Wellington was also prominently associated with the foundation of King's College, London: he owned ten £100 shares and donated £300 to the College. As Prime Minister, he chaired the opening of King's College on 21 June 1828, accompanied by bishops and archbishops – for this was seen as the Christian counterpart to the education offered by University College in 'Godless Gower Street'.

Unfortunately, in certain minds – notably that of trouble-seeking Lord Winchilsea – Wellington's link with this new institution was in danger of spelling out a message of Catholic Emancipation, with easy access both to King's College and the king's Parliament. The earl accused him in the Lords of 'the introduction of Popery into every department of the State'. Such a public attack meant that Wellington felt he had no option but to challenge Winchilsea to the one duel he ever fought in his life (plate 59). The duel was set for the morning of Sunday 21 March 1829 in Battersea

Fields. Wellington fired deliberately wide; Winchilsea fired in the air; his second read from a piece of paper: 'That won't do; it is no apology.' The necessary word, 'sorry', added, the duke bowed, touched his hat, wished everyone 'Good morning' and rode away. It was clearly a duel in which neither side had intended to inflict injury.

It was in 1829 that George IV appointed Wellington Lord Warden of the Cinque Ports – a job that, although unpaid, allowed him to exert plenty of influence. It gave him an official residence: Walmer Castle, near Deal, built by King Henry VIII in the 1540s. Wellington loved Walmer. 'The place is delightful', he wrote to Harriet Arbuthnot in July 1829. He enjoyed entertaining visitors, who included Victoria and Albert with their young family in 1842, and especially playing with the children who came to see him. A telling example of his kindness was shown when he personally delivered a bouquet of flowers to a small girl who was being bullied at her day school in Kensington. Well into old age, Wellington maintained his charisma. The young Benjamin Disraeli commented on the 'gruff, husky sort of downright Montaignish naiveté about him, which is quaint, unusual, and tells.' William Gladstone observed that Wellington 'appears to speak little and never for speaking's sake, but only to convey an idea commonly worth conveying.' Benjamin Haydon, who stayed at Walmer Castle in October 1839 when painting the portrait on which 'The Duke of Wellington surveying the battlefield of Waterloo' is based (see plate 61), recorded in his diary: 'I hit his grand, upright, manly expression. He looked like an eagle who had put on human shape.' There is a touching passage by Thomas Carlyle describing the Duke in these later years:

> *Truly a beautiful old man – I had never seen till now how beautiful; and what an expression of graceful simplicity, veracity and nobleness there is about the old hero when you see him close at hand ... Eyes, beautiful light blue, full of mild valour, with infinitely more faculty and geniality than I had fancied before ... The voice, too, ... is 'aquiline', clear, perfectly equable – uncracked, that is – and perhaps almost musical ... – Eighty-two, I understand. He glided slowly along, slightly saluting this and that other; clear, clean, fresh as this June evening itself ...*

At the age of 83, on 18 June 1852 at Apsley House, Wellington hosted his last annual Waterloo Dinner. Those present included Viscount Hardinge, Sir Harry Smith, Lieutenant-General Lord Fitzroy Somerset (later Lord Raglan), Field Marshal the Marquess of Anglesey (the one-legged former Earl of Uxbridge), and General Sir Peregrine Maitland, Commander of the Guards at Waterloo. As the *Morning Chronicle* reported:

60 People sit on the Lion's Mound, Waterloo, 20 June 2010, during a re-enactment of the 1815 Battle of Waterloo

61 Benjamin Robert Haydon (1786–1846)
Arthur Wellesley, 1st Duke of Wellington, 1839

Oil on canvas
National Portrait Gallery, London

Depicting the ageing Duke surveying the now-peaceful battlefield of Waterloo, Haydon's portrait is a companion to his *Napoleon Musing at St Helena*, 1830 (National Portrait Gallery, London).

62 John William Salter (fl.1848–1875)
The 1836 Waterloo Banquet, 1836
Oil on canvas
Private Collection
The annual Waterloo Dinner at Apsley House 'to the memory of those who fell at the Battle of Waterloo'.

At exactly half-past seven the Duke and the Prince Consort [Prince Albert] *led a column of Wellington's Old Companions in the field into the Waterloo Chamber, still decked with the paintings taken from Joseph's coach at Vitoria ... The Portuguese silver platter, a superb piece of workmanship, with its hundreds of emblematic figures, adorned the great length of the table ... and silver gilt statuettes of the Duke and of Napoleon ...*

Of the 85 people who sat at that table, almost all were survivors of Waterloo. Dinner over, Prince Albert rose to toast the Duke, speaking of his 'delight and satisfaction in seeing our illustrious host in such excellent health and spirits on the present occasion.' While the assembled company drank a toast, the band played 'See the Conquering Hero Comes'. It was then the Duke's turn to speak. Wellington asked everyone to raise their glasses 'to the memory of those who fell at the battle of Waterloo'. Then, one by one, he toasted each of the principal units. Wellington's final toast was to Harry Smith, now General Sir Harry Smith, who had married a Portuguese woman, Juana, during the Peninsular War. They had recently returned from a difficult period governing Cape Colony, but their local popularity never waned, and two towns, Harrismith and Ladysmith, were named after them. When, less than three months after this 1852 Waterloo Dinner, the Duke of Wellington died, Harry Smith was a pallbearer.

Death came on 14 September 1852. At 5.30 on the previous morning Wellington rose – early as usual – to look at his garden, and then spent an enjoyable day at Walmer with Charles's young family. He went to bed in the small room in one of the turrets where he was happiest sleeping on his old camp bed. Shortly after Kendall, his valet, woke him at 6.30 the next morning, Wellington became seriously unwell. When his apothecary, Dr Hulke, arrived at 9am, the Duke passed his hand across his chest and complained of 'some derangement'. Having a small drink of tea only made matters worse. The local doctor was summoned, but Wellington failed to regain consciousness. At 2pm Kendall suggested that they lift him into his favourite wing chair. Seated in this, he made his most understated of manoeuvres, slipping from life into death as though it were to walk a few paces across a battlefield. Dr Hulke's son held a mirror to his mouth. Wellington's own son, Charles, saw the mirror stay bright, unmisted by the breath of life.

During his later years, when Wellington was living at Walmer, he took enormous pleasure in the things that his public role had previously denied him. He enjoyed visits from his growing family and the company of the local children, who evidently felt quite at home in the Castle. At last, the hero of Waterloo, though continuing to serve his country, recaptured something approaching a private life. But the people's response to his death, and the nature of his funeral, proved that he belonged in the end to the nation.

CHAPTER III

A Funeral and a Foundation

63 Louis Haghe (1806–1885)
The Lying in State of the 1st Duke of Wellington, 1852
Lithograph
Wellington College

Wellington had said that he would like to be buried in the churchyard not far from Walmer Castle. 'Where the tree falls, there let it lie', as he put it to his friend George Gleig. But, like Nelson, whose wish to be buried in the family churchyard in Norfolk was ignored, the nation's saviour was given his final resting place in a chilly tomb in St Paul's Cathedral (see plate 64). Parliament voted on £100,000 for the nation's grandest state funeral to date. The man who had spent so many hours of his life on horseback made his final journey in a modern method of transport, which he had never liked: on 14 November 1852, a train took his body to London. He lay in state in the Great Hall of the Royal Chelsea Hospital, where the pensioners now dine (plate 63). The first person who came to pay her respects was, naturally, a very distraught Queen Victoria. Then the crowd surged in her wake, several of these thousands of people dying in the crush. The body was later escorted by the Household Cavalry to Horse Guards, the Duke's former office, in time for a full state funeral the next day – 18 November. Prince Albert had been full of ideas for the design of the funeral car, which was unfortunately much too large and unwieldy to perform as it should (see plate 66). The writer Thomas Carlyle dismissed the Prince Consort's design as the 'abominably ugliest', describing the funeral procession as 'this vile *ne plus ultra* of Cockneyism'. Diarist Charles Greville's verdict on the car was equally harsh: 'tawdry, cumbrous ... contrived by a German artist ... under Prince Albert's direction – no proof of his good taste.' At 21 feet long and 12 feet wide, it weighed 18 tons; the 12 black-clad horses lent by a brewery for the occasion could not stop its wheels getting stuck in the mud on Pall Mall. Sixty policemen, some lassoed with ropes, were needed to drag it free. It required the strength of a posse of sailors to pull the car up the final stretch of Ludgate Hill.

ARTHUR DUKE OF WELLINGTON

FUNERAL-CAR OF THE DUKE OF WELLINGTON.
DESIGNED FROM THE GENERAL IDEA SUGGESTED BY THE SUPERINTENDENTS OF THE DEPARTMENT OF PRACTICAL ART BY THE ART SUPERINTENDENT REDGRAVE, R. A.
THE CONSTRUCTIVE AND ORNAMENTAL DETAILS BY PROFESSOR SEMPER, THE DETAILS RELATING TO WOVEN FABRICS AND HERALDRY BY OCTAVIUS HUDSON, PROFESSOR.

opposite, clockwise

64 *Tomb of the Late Duke of Wellington, in the Crypt of St Paul's Cathedral, London*, 1854
Engraving
Published in the *Illustrated London News*, 4 November 1854

65 George Gammon Adams (1821–1898)
Arthur Wellesley, 1st Duke of Wellington, 1852
Plaster cast of death-mask
National Portrait Gallery, London

66 Richard Redgrave (1804–1888)
View of the Funeral Car of the Duke of Wellington, 1852
Lithograph
Published by Day & Son
Guildhall Art Gallery, London

Once they reached St Paul's Cathedral, their problems were not over: transferring the coffin to the bier at the west door took well over an hour, thanks to the failure of the machinery. Meanwhile the streets were pulsating with more than a million onlookers.

Wellington himself would doubtless have preferred a much simpler send-off. Field Marshal Lord Seaton complained that the interminable reading out of the Duke's titles and the tossing of his broken staff of office into his tomb were 'inapplicable to the present age'. But for the hundreds of thousands of people who witnessed the funeral, the whole ceremony was extremely moving – and perhaps a key instigator of the cult of death and mourning that, following especially on the death of Prince Albert less than nine years later, was to become a feature of the Victorian era. Indeed, Victoria herself possessed a gold bracelet whose chief adornment was a lock of Wellington's hair, taken from his head shortly before the coffin lid was closed (see plate 70); his daughter-in-law Lady Douro was happy to be given the false teeth he was wearing when he died.

A painting of the funeral shows the interior of St Paul's looking as dangerous as the stands of an unmodernised football ground, with crowds of mourners heaving and swelling into every available space of the cathedral, from top to bottom (see plate 68). There they were, leaning forward, straining to catch every note of the death march that sounded as the coffin was lowered into the vault. Those close enough might have caught the gesture of the Marquess of Anglesey, who put out his hand to touch it. Their experience, as they marvelled at the six tall candlesticks that stood guard around the coffin, was repeated more than one hundred years later when these same candles were re-kindled for the funeral of Winston Churchill (plate 67).

67 A candle used at the funerals of the 1st Duke of Wellington and Prime Minister Winston Churchill, 2014

The question of how best to honour the Duke's memory was a concern of the Queen and Prince Consort, along with her Prime Minister, Edward Stanley, Earl of Derby. The three of them met at Balmoral shortly after Wellington's death was announced, to decide on the most suitable memorial. He might, like Nelson, have been awarded a tall monument in some central London square, but Wellington died at a time when education was very much to the forefront of people's minds. It had become apparent that British schools were perhaps being overtaken by their European counterparts in preparing the next generation for the world that was opening up in the second half of the nineteenth century. A new and growing middle class sought an education for their sons that would ease their passage into a society no longer so unremittingly dominated by the aristocracy. The 2nd Duke of Wellington (formerly the Marquess of Douro) opposed the idea of founding a school in his father's memory, favouring instead the erection of a bronze statue of the Duke in every

68 William Simpson (1823–1899) after Louis Haghe (1806–1885)
Interior of St Paul's Cathedral during the funeral of the Duke of Wellington, London, 1852, 1853
Lithograph
Published by Ackermann & Co.
Guildhall Art Gallery, London

town in the country. But his wishes were politely ignored. The Queen and the Prince had plans.

A full account of Wellington College's inception is given in the *Narrative of the Foundation of Wellington College, Compiled by Direction of the Governors*. This was written by Sir Wellington Patrick Talbot, secretary to Lord Derby and to the College Governors. He was responsible for a large slice of the work needed in inviting subscriptions and organising the work of the Governors, eventually becoming a Governor himself. Very soon after Wellington's death, Derby wrote from Downing Street to some of the most influential Members of Parliament:

69 Lover's eye brooch, England, 1790–1810
Gold, pearls, diamonds and painted miniature
Victoria and Albert Museum, London

70 Diamond-set gold bracelet containing a lock of the Duke of Wellington's hair, which he gave to his niece, Lady Emily Wellesley-Pole, 1814. Such mourning bracelets and brooches, containing a lock of the deceased's hair, were popular at the time.

> *The universal desire felt by all classes to do honour to the memory of the Duke of Wellington, will probably lead to the erection of statues and other monuments in many of the principal towns in the kingdom, some of which have indeed already taken steps in this direction. But projects of this description, however much they may contribute to the ornament of the respective localities, and however gratifying they may be to the feelings of their inhabitants, can possess little more than local interest, can be joined in by comparatively few of the population, and are not calculated to confer any substantial benefit upon the community. With a view to erect a Monument to the memory of the Great Duke to which all may contribute, which shall be worthy of its object and of the nation, and which shall be of permanent and important advantage to that service of which he was long the head and the ornament, it is proposed to erect and endow, by public subscription, a School or College, to bear the name of the Duke of Wellington, for the gratuitous, or nearly gratuitous Education of Orphan Children of Indigent and Meritorious Officers of the army ... a class of men peculiarly liable to casualties, by which their families are often left in a condition of the most painful pecuniary embarrassment, and under circumstances in which the necessary stringent regulations of the War Office preclude the possibility of any relief from public funds.*

As the Founders envisaged it, every thousand pounds raised would guarantee an annuity of some £30, sufficient for 'the education of one child'. They recognised that 'a considerable sum' would be required for putting up the building, and proposed to withhold all expenditure until they had raised £100,000.

How were these large amounts of money to be raised? Victoria, Albert and the Earl of Derby all agreed that it should be by public subscription. Letters were sent out to likely donors and advertisements appeared in the papers. These donations were, of course, voluntary – except in the case of the army: every soldier, whatever his rank, had to give up a day's pay to the Duke's memorial, whether he wished to or not. As Talbot records, 'subscriptions flowed in with great rapidity', and the Prince Consort was able to preside over a meeting of principal subscribers held at Buckingham Palace on 3 August 1853. He announced that Her Majesty would be delighted to grant the proposed new institution a Royal Charter and to become its Visitor. She would appoint 30 Governors. The College, according to its Charter, would provide an education for:

> *the children of deceased officers, who may have borne commissions either in Our Royal Army or in the Army of the East India Company ... Such*

71 William Simpson (1823–1899)
The Queen Laying the Foundation Stone of Wellington College, 2 June 1856, 1856
Watercolour
Royal Collection, London

children shall be eligible as candidates, without regard for their religious persuasion or creed, provided they shall have been born in legal wedlock, and, in the estimate of the Governors, shall be in circumstances of need.

These pupils would be given a free education, or charged only a nominal sum. The school would be known as 'The Wellington College'.

The first Governors were headed by Prince Albert, who chaired the Board, and included the Duke of Cambridge, the Archbishop of Canterbury, the Duke of Wellington (the Duke of Wellington, it was decreed in the Charter, would always and automatically be a Governor, although the 2nd Duke remained implacably opposed to the idea of the College until he became its Vice-President), the Marquess of Anglesey, the Earl of Derby, Viscount Hardinge, the Bishop of London and Lord Raglan. These were undoubtedly men distinguished in military and ecclesiastical fields, but possibly with little expertise in either education or finance. They held their first meeting at the Palace of Westminster, Prince Albert (in the Chair) being unanimously elected President, with Derby as Vice-President. The Governors expressed their hope that the subscriptions received so far would, according to Talbot's account, 'lay the foundation of an Institution worthy of the memory of the Great

Duke, and beneficial to the Service of which he was so distinguished an ornament.' So it would appear that at this stage they envisaged The Wellington College – part school, part national monument – as a training ground for future generations of army officers. It is worth remembering that during the 1850s the British army fought the Crimean War and the Indian Mutiny. A quick glance at the Governors' Address to Her Majesty at the inauguration of the College offers a clue supporting the idea that a supply of well-educated officers was very important:

> *It would be too much to hope that it should ever boast of one from among its Pupils who might emulate the fame of the Great Warrior and Statesman in whose honour it has been erected, but we may trust that by the blessing of Almighty God upon its teaching it may send forth many deeply imbued with the lofty principles which regulated his conduct, and prepared, whatever may be their station in life, to follow the great example which he has left of unswerving loyalty to the Throne, of devotion to his country's service, and of strict and unhesitating obedience to the calls of public duty.*

72 Unknown artist
The Inauguration of Wellington College by the Queen – Arrival of Her Majesty at the College, 1859
Engraving
Published in the *Illustrated London News*, 12 February 1859
Wellington College

In her response, Queen Victoria expressed the hope that the pupils of Wellington College would show 'cheerful obedience to those who are set in authority over them' and so 'earn a character for the College worthy of the name it bears'. Her enthusiasm for the Foundation came as no surprise, given her admiration of the late Duke and the fact that her beloved Consort was masterminding the project (see plate 72).

Shortly after the College opened, the writer and local clergyman Charles Kingsley decided to enrol his son Maurice as a pupil (the perhaps surprising presence of a boy who was quite clearly not the orphaned son of an army officer will be explained later). Kingsley was a great admirer of Prince Albert, agreeing wholeheartedly with his emphasis on the study of science. Writing to the late Duke's nephew, Gerald Wellesley, Dean of Windsor, Kingsley expressed the hope that Wellingtonians would say:

73 Otto Herschan (fl.1860–1875)
Charles Kingsley (1819–1875), novelist and Canon of Chester, c.1860

'I am a Wellington boy. I have before me the example of the greatest modern Englishman. His name is written on the walls, his portrait hangs in my room – He shall be my Model. It is a point of honour in me to set him frequently before my eyes, in a School dedicated to his memory, whose motto is Virtutis fortuna comes.' That thought I intend to keep alive in my boy – If the shadow of the Wellington College will foster in him some of the virtues of your illustrious uncle – that will be enough for me.

In replying to the Governors' Address at the inauguration of Wellington College in January 1859, Queen Victoria anticipated that the school would 'furnish the means of a religious, moral and intellectual education of the best description'. This ideal education was initially based on models pioneered by her husband. Indeed, Wellington College was in its beginnings the brainchild of this remarkable man, a product of the German Enlightenment who was described by Disraeli as 'I think the best educated man I ever met'. As children, Albert and his older brother Ernst were taken under the wing of Baron Christian Frederick Stockmar, adviser to Albert's Uncle Leopold, who, in the words of A.N. Wilson, created 'a monarch for the modern age'. The education Stockmar plotted out for the Saxe-Coburg princes was conventionally based on a knowledge of languages, mathematics and literature, but also included economics, agriculture, architecture and art. Albert studied in Italy and became a passably good painter, with a connoisseur's eye for art collecting (he picked up a drawing by Albrecht Dürer and a portrait by Anthony Van Dyck during a trip to the Rhine), and was an extremely talented musician, who composed some fine *Lieder*. He also studied in Brussels, a centre of liberal and democratic ideas. Stockmar decided to send Ernst and Albert to the University of Bonn in 1837, dismissing Berlin University as an institution that might make them 'formal and priggish'. In Bonn, Albert studied law, government, philosophy and history, 'all subjects', as Wellington College's historian and one-time Master, David Newsome, observed in his centennial history of the school, 'about which Oxford and Cambridge knew little and taught less.' He continues:

He was not long in England before he developed a dislike of narrow classical scholarship ... He marvelled at the ignorance of the English; ignorance which was damaging to their industrial and cultural future, for it rendered them even more insular than they were by nature, and therefore in the long run materially less powerful, since the nation must sink beneath the scientific achievements of its continental competitors ...

This attitude is crucial to an understanding of what Prince Albert hoped Wellington College would offer by way of an education.

BAILEY RAWLINS' EXPANDING VIEW OF THE GREAT EXHIBI- TION
THE NAVE
PRINTED IN COLORS, AND PUBLISHED
FOR THE PROPRIETOR, BY CHAS MOODY, 257, HIGH HOLBORN

74 Bailey Rawlins
Expanding View of the Great Exhibition, 1851
Colour lithograph with watercolour
Printed and published by Charles Moody, London, 1851
Victoria and Albert Museum, London

75 Joseph Nash (1809–1878)
The Indian Court at the Great Exhibition, 1851
Colour lithograph
Published by Dickinson Brothers, London, 1854
Victoria and Albert Museum, London

Here was a man with a vision and a mission. His Royal Highness's vision, which among other things included an emphasis on the study of the political and natural sciences, bore little resemblance to conventional English educational models. This meant that, unfortunately, it did not always accord with that of the first Master of Wellington (whom Albert was instrumental in appointing), Edward White Benson. The Prince's greatest legacy during his lifetime was probably the Great Exhibition of 1851, which championed innovations in science and technology (see plates 74 and 75). Benson was a classical scholar and future Archbishop of Canterbury. There are those who believe that Prince Albert had it in mind that the school would become a German-style military academy, whereas Benson wished to model it on Rugby, where he taught classics before going to Wellington. Of course, just because he was German does not mean that Albert was fixated on all things military and disciplinarian. We also associate German culture – both then and now – with music and literature, philosophy and technology. What is beyond doubt, however, is that the uniform Albert designed for the boys of Wellington College (it was dropped a few years after he died) had the distinct look of a soldier boy from some obscure and eccentric regiment: dark green, with brass buttons and, as Newsome describes it, 'plaid trousers and a postman's cap with red lines and a gilt crown set in front ... suggestive of railway employees' (plate 76).

76 Charles Cubitt (Beresford 1859–1864) appears to have adapted the official original uniform for the purposes of a portrait photograph. Senior boys seem to take increasing liberties until the abolition of the uniform.
Wellington College
Accepted to Christ Church Oxford, Cubitt became the first Wellingtonian to gain entrance to university.

What Albert wanted to avoid above all else was a uniform resembling academic gowns or church robes. This style was anathema to the Prince, who abhorred any sense of the monastic lingering over Britain's schools – a bias that had an important influence on his vision for Wellington's architecture too. He also disliked standard English public school practices such as masters (other than the Headmaster) and prefects using the cane, fagging, and too much chapel on a Sunday. He was keen that the school should not be too large. This sounds an enlightened idea, although it created problems for Wellington College that have never quite been resolved: his belief that the maximum number of pupils in a school should be 250 meant that the Hall (now Old Hall) and Great School were not built on a sufficiently large scale.

Determined to shift the new school away from the traditional British model, Albert sent Benson, soon after his appointment and the year before Wellington opened, on a tour of Europe. He was to examine in particular a group of German schools that the Prince thought would give him some ideas for Wellington's educational philosophy. Unfortunately, a list of these schools has not survived. All we do know is that Benson returned to England more convinced than ever that his own country had all the right answers as far as education was concerned.

Albert, meanwhile, was determined that the English should go against the grain and try something new, seeing beyond Greek, Euclid and the Church Catechism, and that Wellington College – unlike traditional schools such as Rugby or Eton – should prepare its pupils for life in the world, rather than life at university. Despite their philosophical differences, Benson greatly admired his President, whom he described as 'a prince of princes', recognising that he had put before him a courageous and visionary plan for the school, and that in his 'Wellington Testimonial' Albert was its true Founder. When Charles Kingsley wrote to Gerald Wellesley he cited four reasons as to why he was sending his son to the new college: '1) Because he will not be stupefied with Latin and Greek. 2) Because there are no traditions there. 3) Because it costs £100 instead of £300. 4) Because it is under the Superintendence of the Prince Consort.' Impressed by the concern Albert showed for the school, Kingsley added, 'Long may he live to interfere therein!'

77 William Edward Kilburn (1818–1891)
Prince Albert, 1848
Hand-coloured daguerreotype
Royal Collection, London

Albert's educational philosophy is perhaps best indicated by the ideas behind the Great Exhibition. This was inspired by the Paris Exhibition of two years earlier (1849) and displayed British achievements in the arts, science and technology. Its ethos suggested that intellectual excellence should be allowed to produce practical and wealth-creating outcomes. Appealing for subscriptions, he wrote, 'The distances which separated the nations are rapidly vanishing before the achievements of modern invention, and we can traverse them with incredible ease ... The publicity of the present day causes that no sooner is a discovery made than it is already improved upon and surpassed by competing efforts.' Albert used the £18,000 profit generated by the Great Exhibition to build a permanent exhibition centre in South Kensington, which still stands today (and includes the Victoria and Albert Museum, the Natural History Museum, and others) as proof of this extraordinary man's legacy as a patron of art, science and lifelong learning. He also brought out into the light of day paintings that had been languishing in the vaults of Hampton Court, planned the construction of Osborne House on the Isle of Wight, created a model dairy at Windsor and a model housing development in Kennington, and generally introduced to public life the message of the new enlightenment – that every man, woman and child could partake of the riches of national culture.

But if the Prince Consort provided the vision, it was Prime Minister Lord Derby (a scholar in his own right, who had translated Homer's *The Iliad*) and Sir Wellington Patrick Talbot who carried out most of the hard work in raising the subscriptions that would make the school financially viable. Talbot, son-in-law to Derby, godson to the late Duke and author of the *Narrative of the Foundation*, helped to send out the Appeal for Subscriptions. Curiously, they appear to have used a system that differs very little from the one familiar to us in the era just prior to the advent of online donations: 'Should you approve of the proposed project, you are requested to subscribe your name to the inclosed Form; insert the sum which it is your intention to subscribe; and direct it to the Hon. W.P. Talbot, 10, Downing Street, London.' The chief difference, of course, was that donors were not being invited to enclose the money, but rather a commitment to give a certain sum. This created problems later when the cash was being counted, as we shall see. By the middle of 1853 the letter making this request for subscriptions had been sent to at least 100,000 people – to every Member of both Houses, to 'Civic Dignitaries throughout the Kingdom' (as the *Narrative* puts it), to the Heads of all the Oxford and Cambridge colleges, to clergymen, army officers, the Governor-General of India, the Governors of a number of colonies and 'the Commanding officer of every Regiment in Her Majesty's Service'. Advertisements were also placed in all the main newspapers. Subscribers were invited to offer whatever they could afford, from a pound to sums in the thousands.

Talbot was able to report to the meeting of principal subscribers on 3 August 1853 that £80,000 had been promised by the British, with at least £20,000 expected from India. So in theory the required £100,000 had been met. Talbot later worked with Lieutenant-Colonel H. Grove in November 1856 on the *Alphabetical List of Subscribers to a Memorial of the Duke of Wellington*, published by Her Majesty's Stationery Office the following year. Explaining in an introductory note that army officers, whose orphaned children would be the beneficiaries of the subscribers' generosity, were 'particularly liable to be cut off suddenly, and in too many instances leave their families totally unprovided for', Grove and Talbot went on to list the name of every single subscriber to the Wellington College foundation appeal. Heading the list, 'Her Most Gracious Majesty' was shown to have donated £1,500, followed by 'His Royal Highness Prince Albert', who gave £750. The King of the Belgians gave £200, the Duchess of Kent £300. Beneath the list of royal names, a rather more unconventional donation is recorded:

> *As a most interesting incident the following is placed in this conspicuous position. It is a donation of 250 rupees* [valued at the time at £250] *from the survivors of the troops of the Berar-Nagpore State, who fought in the Deccan Campaign in 1803, against General Wellesley. Half a century after the event have these gallant Eastern warriors paid the tribute of respect to the illustrious Commander by whom they were vanquished.*

There follows a List of The Army and Foreign Stations – companies, regiments, battalions and the like – that subscribed. Then, in the General List, individual donors are named in alphabetical order. It makes for interesting reading. Eight Beresfords offered donations, ranging from £1 from two Lieutenants to £500 from Viscount Beresford. The Dean Chapter of Rochester gave the rather strange sum of £4.3s.3d. The Duke of Richmond, descendant of the host of the eve of Waterloo ball in Brussels, gave £100. A 'Widow of a General Officer' gave £1, the Rajah of Nagpore £1,000, the King of Oude £300 and Moung Van Oer, Writer, £2. The range of donors, and of the sums subscribed, testify to the high regard in which the late Duke was held across all parts of society, both at home and in the colonies.

For the sake of the orphans selected for this new enterprise, the school now needed to be organised according to a workable pattern. It was decided that boys who applied for admission to the college would be chosen by the Governors at a special six-monthly meeting. They agreed that no boys under the age of 11 or over 13 would be admitted, and they would not be allowed to remain at the college beyond the age of 16. The plan was to have three classes, with 20 boys in each class. The 20 boys in the First Class would pay £10 a year each; the annual charge for the 20 boys in the Second Class would be £15 each; and in the Third Class they would pay £20. According to the *Narrative*, the Governors decided that, as well as the original 60 boys, 'an additional number of boys might be received into the School without, in all probability, any addition to the staff or any increase in the established charges. Resolved, therefore, – That a Fourth Class of forty boys be admitted at an annual payment of £30 for each boy.' The Governors were emboldened to add that 'Inasmuch as the payments for the boys in the Fourth Class will more than defray the whole expense of their maintenance and clothing, it is conceived that there can be no objection to receive into the Class boys, not orphans, the sons of officers serving in the Army, giving the preference, however, to orphans.'

Already, the original concept of the Foundation was being tampered with, although the enlargement of the school from its original small size, and a less rigid selection formula, could to an extent be justified. Certainly the Governors believed that this 'extension ... would be highly beneficial to the School, and would confer a great benefit on the Service by supplying a want long felt by officers in the Army, and for which they have unsuccessfully attempted to provide by their own unaided efforts.' In other words, the school that had so far never existed – one for the sons of *living* officers – would spring to life and be enthusiastically embraced by a grateful army.

The grand concept continued to mutate. At a Governors' meeting on 27 February 1857 it was agreed that £40 a year should be charged for 'the education of boys in the Fourth Class, or non-Foundationers'. Then, when they met on 18 November 1858, the Governors decided that:

in addition to the 100 boys to be admitted on the opening of the College, viz. eighty-one Foundationers and nineteen Non-Foundationers, a further number of 100 boys should be admitted as Non-Foundationers, to consist of the sons of officers and of the sons of civilians, the preference to be given to the sons of officers, the former to pay £70 a year and the latter £100 a year.

So they had come a long way from the original vision of Wellington College as a school purely for orphans. They had moved from taking the orphaned sons of officers to the sons of living officers to the sons of civilians. It was not until a Royal Commission looked into this change in policy in 1880 that the anomaly received its most serious challenge.

From the opening of the College in 1859 until 1863 all Foundationers were given, free of charge, 'two suits of clothing and ... a great coat once in two years, the annual cost of which to the College was £6'. In 1867, six years after his death, Prince Albert's unprepossessing uniform was abandoned, at which point 'the cost of the clothing supplied to each Foundationer was increased to £8.3s.6d, owing to three suits of uniform being supplied annually instead of two and to the discontinuance of the supply of great coats'. So we can see that even the minutiae of expenses incurred by school uniform were not considered too trivial for the Governors' consideration. They briefly discussed funding a school for girls. It would have had to be a separate establishment, of course, as all such schools at that time were single sex, but sadly not enough money had been raised to make this possible.

Religious education and worship were to be 'according to the doctrines and principles of the Church of England', but, added the Governors, 'attendance on such worship or teaching shall not be required of boys whose guardians may object on the grounds of religious dissent' – an interesting signifier of nineteenth-century enlightenment. When considering the curriculum, Governors specified:

1st. What is usually understood by a good English and Classical Education [here they were playing the conventional card]; *2ndly. Those branches of scientific knowledge which have a special application to the Arts, Commerce, and Industry of the Country* [here we see the influence of the Prince Consort]; *3rdly. The Modern Languages* [the Prince Consort again].

It was also stipulated, naturally, that 'the Masters selected be men skilled severally in these departments of instruction.'

Unfortunately, once builders' tenders had been analysed in July 1855, the Governors (who had not themselves been able to benefit from the rounded education they hoped to offer at Wellington College) found the sums did not add up. It was estimated that a total of £55,000 was still required, but only £29,000 was available. So 'it was determined that a further appeal should be made to the public for subscription'. It fell to Vice-President Derby to draw up the appeal, which was advertised in the newspapers in graphically heart-rending terms:

> *At a time when public sympathy is deeply engaged on behalf of those gallant men, of all ranks, who are freely shedding their blood in their country's cause, or falling victim to the fatal disease of whose ravages we have recently had the most melancholy proof, the Governors of the Wellington College, for the education of orphan sons of officers in the military service of the Crown or East India Company, deem it their duty to call the attention of the country to the state and prospects of the Institution for which they are trustees, and earnestly to solicit for its continued and increased support ...*
>
> *Beyond the very moderate pittance of the Widows' Pension, and the occasional aid of the Compassionate Fund, no provision whatever is made from public or private sources; and yet, among them are to be found ... the severest forms of distress and suffering. The family of the officer who dies in the field or in the hospital, are deprived not only of the income which they might have derived from his pay, but lose the whole sum which, in most cases, he had invested in the purchase of his commission; and from a state of comparative ease are too often plunged into one of destitution, the more painful from the struggle to conceal the intensity of suffering, and to maintain something of the appearance of their former condition ...*
>
> *The Governors will not for a moment believe that when war and disease are daily adding fearfully to the number of claimants on such a charity, the British public ... will turn a deaf ear to their urgent appeal.*

Donations by annual subscription were invited. 'I am still busily employed in dinning the Public for the remainder', wrote Talbot in March 1855. 'Indeed I am almost ashamed to appear in London for I am sure people must consider me a public nuisance.' By December 1855, this additional appeal had raised between £5,000 and £6,000 – only a small proportion of the sum needed to make up funds to the required £55,000. So the Building Committee suggested that the furnishing and fittings of the two upper Dormitories 'should for the present be dispensed with'. It was also decided that the Chapel and the infirmary could not, for the time being, be constructed.

While the Founders were fortunate in the purchase of the Wellington College site, there had been a few false starts: for example, at one point the possibility was considered of erecting the school in the grounds of the Royal Hospital, Chelsea, in what had been the Governor's Garden, but it transpired that this piece of land was intended as a burial site. As MP Sidney Herbert commented: 'Chelsea is not a healthy place ... and the population around it is of the worst description.' A Mr Allcock of Banstead offered a generous number of acres on the Downs at Banstead. This was the site favoured by Prince Albert. But Mr Allcock's neighbour, Lord Egremont, mounted fierce opposition to the plan, complaining that a school on his doorstep would have a very adverse effect on his privacy.

Eventually, on 21 November 1854, the Governors agreed that they should close with Mr Robert Gibson, who offered them 12 acres, free of charge, from his estate near Sandhurst, in the parish of Wokingham. Prince Albert and the Building Committee had visited the site on 5 April and found it eminently suitable. In addition to the 12 original acres offered, they decided to purchase from Mr Gibson a further 100 acres at £10 an acre, 'at which moderate price', Talbot tells us, 'Mr Gibson was

78 'Wellingtonia' Redwoods on North Front, Wellington College, 2013

willing to sell'. At first glance the location might have seemed disadvantageous: during the previous century the area on and around Bagshot Heath was a known haunt of highwaymen. In his 150th anniversary history of the College, Patrick Mileham quotes Daniel Defoe on the subject: 'A vast track of land ... given to barrenness, horrid and frightful to look on, not only good for little, but good for nothing ... a great black desert.' *The Times*, in an article published two days after the formal inauguration of Wellington College in Great School on 29 January 1859, commented on 'the bleak, inhospitable looking moor on which the building has unfortunately been erected', regretting that 'a spot so desolate and cold' had been chosen.

In fact the site had many advantages. As David Newsome explains in his 1959 history, 'It was a convenient location for obtaining building materials – bricks and sand, gravel and grit. There was good water to be had at a depth of some twelve to twenty feet. Also ... it was conveniently close to a railway line, albeit only a branch line from Reigate to Reading.' The reason the land was so cheap – indeed the reason also for the construction of Broadmoor (in 1863) and the creation of Bracknell new town (in 1949) in the same area – was that it was of poor quality, marshy in places, and could not be farmed. Notice that the name 'Crowthorne' does not appear in the mid-nineteenth-century discussion of the site. The village was to follow on later – and, as Newsome points out, once Crowthorne and Broadmoor were established, the land rose considerably in value: when Governors purchased an additional 150 acres in 1863–64, they paid £40 an acre.

Despite its barrenness, this stretch of countryside soon attracted enthusiasts. Edward White Benson's son, Arthur C. Benson, recalled how:

79 R. Norman Shaw (1831–1912)
Royal Academy Prize (Architectural Design), Design for a Wellington College, 1853
Engraving
Published in the *Illustrated London News*, 31 December 1853

80 The red-brick Palladian architecture of Wellington College from South Front, 2013

> *You could step out of the College gates, and walk for hours among the red-shafted aisles* [of the pine woods], *with the soft carpet of fir needles, in roads of grey sand, with the wind rustling in the thick foliage at the top ... The air of the whole place was always singularly fresh.*

Indeed, one of the reasons Charles Kingsley decided to send his son to Wellington was 'the physical healthiness of the place ... I like the healthfulness of the soil; the airiness of the situation; the entourage of wild forest, in which the boys may have unlimited bodily freedom'.

William Burn, an architect who inspected the site in December 1854, suggested that the building, when constructed, should have an approach and entrance 'on the north and north-east, and the principal front face towards the south and south-west, occupying a most important position and commanding rich and extensive views, with Stratfieldsaye [*sic*] in the distance'. Although Burn was not the architect who designed the College, his advice was followed: we approach it, entering through Great Gate, along North Front, whereas much of the activity of the school, its 'front face', takes place along South Front.

An edifice 'simple, chaste and classic in character, the Palladian style of architecture' is what Burn recommended. He offered his inspection and advice free of charge, but did not have the time to design the building himself. Instead, he suggested John Shaw (1803–1870), architect of the Royal Naval School at New Cross (now Goldsmiths' College, University of London), where Prince Albert had laid the foundation stone in 1843. His father, also called John Shaw, had designed Christ's Hospital. Constructed from warm red brick, the Royal Naval School and Wellington College are both a striking contrast to the Victorian gothic that was rearing up all around them at the time, and this was a chief reason why Prince Albert favoured Shaw as the project's architect (see plate 80). As with his views on school uniform, anything suggestive of the medieval, including pre-Reformation archways and cloisters, was out of aesthetic bounds. His aim, he declared, was 'to avoid the monastic association'. Rollo St Clair Talboys, in his history of the College, *A Victorian School*, believes that Shaw 'turned deliberately away from Camelot towards the châteaux of the Loire, with perhaps a backward glance at the orangery at Hampton Court ... he desired for him a commemorative building such as the Duke himself would have found familiar'.

So we are not surprised that, viewing the College's construction in September 1858, *The Times* described it as a 'comfortable-looking' building, whose 'cheering presence gives animation to the heaths around; it imparts an air of hospitality to the bleak-looking wolds, and lights up with its ruddy, cheerful glow the sombre pine-woods which surround it.' An early Wellingtonian, Henry Richards, acknowledged that 'the buildings show the mark of the Prince Consort's devoted and untiring mind'. It was Albert who, at a Governors' meeting in November 1858, announced that statues of Wellington's most important Generals would be placed in the eight niches on the north and south fronts of the College (see plates 80 and 81). Relatives and representatives had agreed to donate funds for statues of the Marquess of Anglesey, Lord Beresford, Lord Hill, Lord Hopetoun, Lord Lynedoch, Sir George Murray and the Prince of Orange. His Royal Highness would donate a statue of Field Marshal Blücher. The bust of the Duke of Wellington himself, which looks down from a great height into Front Quad, was designed by Walter James Wyatt (see plate 100).

The Building Committee, in engaging Shaw for the job, recommended that 'a portion only of the building – sufficient to accommodate 100 boys – should, in the first instance, be proceeded with, at an estimated cost of £20,000'. Clearly, worries about cash flow were very much to the fore. At the beginning of July 1855, analysing tenders for the work, the Building Committee decided to go with Messrs H. and R. Holland, whose tender of £36,175 was the lowest. Realising that this sum did not include 'the cost of the chapel, infirmary, water supply, warming apparatus, and laying out the grounds', it was at this point that the Governors concluded they would have to launch the additional appeal to the public.

81 A view of Old Hall and the West Tower from South Front, 2013

For the College's situation within its grounds, the key characteristics of Shaw's plan were the Kilometre – the straight, tree-lined drive up to the College running from east to west – and the transformation of the marshy ground to the north into an ornamental lake. A Mr William Menzies, Deputy Ranger of Windsor Park and therefore well known to Prince Albert, supervised the work on the grounds. He became a Wellington College parent when his son joined the school.

The original 1859 buildings consisted of North Front, including Great Gate and two long colonnaded wings, four storeys each, which extended right the way through the College as it then existed; Great School, where the boys received most of their lessons; and the Hall (now called Old Hall), where they had their dinner. 'On either side', as Mileham describes it, 'massive twin towers ... rise to 95 feet above the ground'. The red brick, made locally, is given extra definition by the Bath stone around the windows. How curious – when one considers this warm colouring and features such as the circular windows – that the national memorial to the man who defeated the French should look so like a French château. But then the Prince Consort probably recognised that the Duke would have felt much more at home in such a setting than in the gloomy monasticism of the gothic revival. The style of the architecture has certainly been described as 'Louis Quinze', and even compared to a Spanish convent. Talboys calls it 'Nineteenth-century Baroque'. In his opinion, Shaw was 'assuredly a craftsman of spirit and of a certain inconsequent gaiety, such as is made visible in his building, and which has infected, it may be, those who have lived in it.'

Nikolaus Pevsner's verdict makes it 'By far the best of these major High Victorian buildings of Berkshire, and one of the most disciplined in its layout and most consistent in its stylistic apparatus.' Pevsner comments on the French influence and also that of Hampton Court, where the quadrangle designed by Sir Christopher Wren for William and Mary resembles the Combermere Quad at Wellington College. This is what is now known as the 'Wrenassaince' style of architecture.

Despite its architectural merits, however, the building has not always worked very effectively as a school. Benson, arriving as the first Master when everything was still sparkling new, quickly found that aesthetics had been achieved at the cost of practical considerations. Indeed the Revd C.W. Penny, who was the College Bursar, as well as an assistant master under Benson, remarked that the design 'is certainly about the worst that could have been chosen for a school in respect to its internal possibilities of convenient arrangement'.

Whatever the subsequent complaints, on the day that the foundation stone was laid it was all smiles and rejoicing. It had originally been intended that the event should take place on 1 May, the Duke's birthday, but the weather had been extremely wet and the ground was far too soggy for the ceremony. So it was delayed until 2 June 1856. As Queen Victoria recorded in her journal (Royal Archives, 2 June 1856):

> *Most fortunately for the day's proceedings ... it was a beautiful warm day ... At ½ p. 11 we started with the 7 Children, our 2 guests* [the Regent of Baden and Prince Friedrich Wilhelm of Prussia, soon to be engaged to her daughter Princess Vicky], *their suites, & all our people, including the D^ss: of Sutherland & the Officers of State. Albert, & all the Gentlemen, in uniform* [Albert as a Field Marshal], *& the Boys in full Highland dress. We went by the South Western Railway & proceeded on to near where the College is to be erected, on an eminence*

82 Bird's-eye view of Wellington College, 2006

> *between Blackwater & Sandhurst College, – a fine position. On leaving the train got into our carriages, Albert & I, driving with the Princes, & Vicky, Alice, & Arthur, & the D^{ss}: of Sutherland, in the 2nd. carriage … The guards lined the road, & George, in command of the troops (for the day) met us on the road, which was very heavy from the previous rain. All the Members of the Commission met us at the Pavilion, & when every-one had arrived, we proceeded, in procession, Albert leading me, Vicky coming next, leading dear little Arthur, to the spot where the ceremony was to take place. The stones or piers of the interior of the building, which was closed in, with spectators, were already standing. Here I received the Address, which L^{d}: Derby read beautifully, to which I read an answer in return. Then the stone was duly laid by me, after the Archbishop of Canterbury had offered up a Prayer, & 3 cheers were given. We returned to the Pavilion, where after a few minutes we sat down to a luncheon of 70 (the 3 younger children lunching alone). All the Children looked very nice, the 4 girls in white muslin dresses, with dark blue sashes. After luncheon we walked through the court on to a Terrace, immediately below which, the troops who had been present, were drawn up. After some delay they began marching past, in quick time, & then, supported by Artillery skirmished, & fired volleys. It was a very fine sight …*

One of the many charming things about this account is the sheer delight the Queen took in what was evidently a very enjoyable day out for the family. The royal party completed most of their journey to the site by train (although doubtless not one they shared with members of the public). It was a particularly significant event as it was the first public appearance of her third son, Prince Arthur, namesake and godson of the late Duke. Judging by the watercolour illustration of the laying of the foundation stone, what appeared to dominate the scene was not so much the stone as the large, scarlet awning (the 'Pavilion', as Her Majesty describes it), supported by four poles (see plate 71).

'May it please Your Majesty', declared Vice-President the Earl of Derby, addressing the Queen on behalf of all the Governors:

We, Your Majesty's most dutiful subjects, the Vice-President and Governors of the Wellington College, approach Your Majesty with the assurance of our devoted loyalty and affectionate attachment to Your Majesty's Throne and Person, and with the expression of our heartfelt gratitude ...

When, upon the death of the late illustrious Duke of Wellington, the country was anxious to testify its deep veneration for his memory, and only doubtful how best to give effect to the general feeling, Your Majesty was graciously pleased at once to adopt (if indeed it may not be truly said that the idea originated in Your Majesty's own mind) the suggestion of combining with a building, of which the architectural character should be worthy of the occasion, an Institution which should perpetuate the name of the great deceased in conjunction with a permanent endowment in favour of the service to which he owed his fame, and on which he has conferred imperishable lustre.

Surrounded by all the blessings of domestic life, which Your Majesty well knows how to prize far above the splendours of a Throne, Your Majesty's maternal heart could sympathise with those less fortunate mothers, whose lot it might be to look with anxiety upon a rising family, orphaned in their country's service, and doomed to struggle with all the evils of severe and, above all, uneducated poverty. An Institution which should mitigate these evils, should soothe these anxieties, should shelter, protect, and educate these orphans, was the monument which Your Majesty invited the country to raise to the lasting memory of the Great Duke.

Lord Derby continued in this vein and concluded with the hope that Her Majesty's 'happy reign' would always be associated with 'the glory and patriotism of Wellington, ... the greatest man of his age'. Victoria then delivered her answer:

There could not be a more worthy record of a country's gratitude to its greatest soldier, than a permanent endowment for the protection and education of the orphans of brave men, whose lives have been laid down in the service of which he was the chief ornament and pride ...

I can express no better wish for my own son, who bears the name of

83 Franz Xaver Winterhalter (1804–1873)
Prince Albert, Prince Consort, unknown date
Mezzotint
Wellington College

that great man [Prince Arthur] *that he should take as his guide through life the example of one with whom it will ever be his high distinction to be connected.*

Certainly Prince Arthur, later the Duke of Connaught, had a long and fruitful connection with his godfather's memorial. He was President of Wellington College from his mother's death in 1901 until his own in 1942. There is a particularly fascinating painting connected with him: *The First of May 1851* by one of Prince Albert's favourite artists, Franz Xaver Winterhalter. The original is at Windsor, but a copy hangs at the College in Old Hall. It is hard to say who exactly is the subject of this painting, which has the iconography of a Nativity scene. The Duke of Wellington is kneeling at the front of the picture, like one of the Magi. He is presenting

84 Copy after Franz Xaver Winterhalter (1804–1873)
The First of May 1851, 1851
Oil on canvas
Wellington College
The Duke of Wellington presenting a christening gift to Victoria and Albert's third son, Prince Arthur. 1 May was the shared birthday of the Duke and the young Prince, and also the opening date of the Great Exhibition (in the background). The original of the painting hangs at Windsor Castle.

85 The foundation stone in Front Quad dates from 1856 and carries the monograms of Queen Victoria and her son, King Edward VII. The Latin inscription translates as: 'Here offer praise to God for all that is given to you'.

what seems to be a precious gift to the baby at the centre of the painting, who sits like the infant Jesus on his mother's lap. The Virgin Mary is, however, none other than that champion of motherhood and family life, Queen Victoria. The baby, who is offering lilies, the symbol of peace, to his godfather, is Prince Arthur. *The First of May*, the picture's title, was the Duke's birthday. Meanwhile, at the back of the painting, standing in a shadow, is the Joseph equivalent, Prince Albert. He is looking at neither of the Arthurs. Instead, as we follow his gaze, we see, way in the distance, his great creation, the Crystal Palace, which, like his featured son, was born in 1851. The Prince Consort appears to have no role in this family scene: his mind is elsewhere.

As the College prepared to open, accommodation for staff and pupils was put in place. The Headmaster (subsequently known simply as 'The Master') was to live on site in his own house or apartment. The original Master's Lodge was situated by Great Gate, where the Housemaster of the Blücher now lives. The assistant masters (three or five in number when the College opened – sources differ) were to have rooms in the College, each with a bedroom and sitting room; they took their meals in the Common Room. There was also a rota requiring them to eat certain meals with the pupils. Talbot observes, 'The case of a Master desiring to marry does not appear to have been contemplated.' Benson was engaged to be married when he joined the College as Headmaster, but it looked as if he might be presiding over a cohort of permanent bachelors.

In the days when Wellington was founded, it was common practice for direct payment to be made to a master as a kind of rent and board, thus enabling pupils to be a boarder in his particular House – or 'Dormitory'. This private arrangement was not, however, part of the grand scheme initially, maybe because of the charitable nature of the Foundation. The first three Dormitories, all of course named after men who had fought alongside Wellington, were the Anglesey, the Blücher and the Beresford. An early Wellington pupil, Augustus Hornby, described a typical Dormitory thus: 'Every boy had an individual, undivided "castle". The cubicle was about eight foot square, with a single iron bed ... A single window, single gas jet above the desk, a perforated banquette admitting a warm and appreciated gush of air, completed my "home".' Hornby's first supper consisted of bread and butter, cheese and 'a very good small beer'. After they had eaten their supper, the boys had an evening service, and lights out was at 10pm.

Talbot records that, in addition to constructing houses for the Headmaster, the Steward, the Bookseller and a number of others, together with a bookshop and confectioner's, the College rented out parts of its estate for building. This was done on 99-year leases at £10 an acre 'to private Gentlemen, for the purpose of building houses for their own occupation, with the privilege of sending their children to the College as Day Boys'. They also sold plots to masters at the college 'for the erection of Boarding Houses, on ... terms approved by the Governors.' We can see that both these developments represented a move away from the original principles. No longer simply a charitable Foundation for the orphaned sons of officers, Wellington College was taking in (as indeed the Governors had realised they would need to do, as a financial necessity) paying civilians. The Dormitories had become Boarding Houses, and so a useful source of income for the masters who took payment for them.

86 John Mayall (1813–1901)
Queen Victoria and Prince Albert, 1861
Daguerreotype

In 1857, Queen Victoria and Prince Albert drove over to Wellington in a phaeton to see how the building work was progressing and, while they were there, enjoy a picnic. It would certainly appear that there was something festive in the way the royal couple viewed this project. The College opened on 20 January 1859. Its pupils on that first day amounted to 76: 47 Foundationers and 29 fee-paying Non-Foundationers. On 29 January, the Queen visited, formally inaugurating the College. Her visit, like those of all Wellington College's Visitors (always the monarch of the day), is marked on a stone by Great School (see plate 85). She made a thorough inspection of the building, then signed the rules and regulations. There was an address from the Governors and a response from Her Majesty. The mood, despite the time of year, was celebratory. Five years later Victoria made her next visit to Wellington: by then she was a widow. It must have been painful to return to a place which was, in many ways, the brainchild of her late husband, and where they had spent some happy hours together, perhaps looking not only at the future of this great school but also at the future they planned to spend with one another.

CHAPTER IV

Benson: the Beginning

87 Unknown artist
Edward White Benson (1829–1896), 1st Master of Wellington College
Wellington College

One of the most important decisions the Prince Consort made as Wellington College came into being was in the choice of its first Master – or Headmaster, as he was initially called. While Prince Albert and the Revd Edward White Benson did not always see eye to eye on matters of education, there is no doubt that the first Master found in his royal sponsor a loyal supporter: 'I cannot express', he wrote to the Dean of Windsor in April 1858, shortly after his appointment, 'how much I am beholden to him, for I feel that certain great difficulties have vanished from the headmaster's path.' It is because he felt so encouraged by the Prince that Benson was willing to put aside six or seven weeks to visiting German schools, as requested. When it came to embedding the educational philosophy of Wellington College in its early days, although Prince Albert might indeed be described as its Founder, it was Benson who had the more lasting influence. The latter was eager to make Wellington College a place of scholarship, which did not entirely tally with the Prince's vision of 'aiming not at the universities but directly at life'. Benson wished to include boys from non-military backgrounds too: were not they also entitled to share in the legacy of the great Duke? Rollo St Clair Talboys concludes: 'In the final issue, and perhaps aided by the Prince's early death, Benson's will prevailed.'

There were other differences. The Prince – and also his Queen – disliked too much time being spent on a Sunday on religious services, while the Revd Benson favoured an exclusively religious and observant Sabbath. But there can be no doubt that, as the first Master, when the College was still being literally as well as philosophically constructed, Benson was the beneficiary of generous outlays in finance and in hours worked by Prince Albert. As well as organising William Theed's busts and statues of Wellington's Generals, he donated 400 books to its library. He contributed to all appeals and financed an annual prize.

The Prince Consort and Governors of the nascent Wellington College relied almost exclusively, in choosing Benson, on the recommendation of William Temple, a former Schools Inspector and the newly appointed Headmaster of Rugby. He had only recently become Head there and, as he explained in a letter to Prince Albert's private secretary, he needed a little more time to observe closely this young schoolmaster. On 20 February 1858, he was able to report of Benson:

> *He seems to me to possess that union of originality and elasticity which is absolutely necessary for working a new scheme. He is intellectually a very superior man; a first rate scholar, and a very fair mathematician. He is one of the best teachers I have ever met with, and this is a very rare qualification, and peculiarly rare when combined with high attainments such as his.*

Benson was only in his late 20s, but Temple pointed out that 'youth has its advantages. The Wellington College will demand a mind singularly free from the prejudices which almost invariably seize upon those who have become accustomed to a settled routine.'

Charles Grey, the recipient of this letter, wrote to the College Governors advising them on the Prince Consort's behalf to accept Temple's recommendation. He asked Lord John Russell to approve the opening of negotiations between the Prince and Benson, to be conducted through Temple. It would be a good idea to identify as soon as possible the new

88 An outside reading lesson, *c.*1910
Wellington College

89 South Front as it appeared before landscaping and the addition of the east and west wings, 1859
Wellington College

Headmaster, who would be in consultation as to the 'fittings of the College'. It was a relief to find Benson; earlier recruitment attempts had garnered a shortlist of four whose attributes, according to Prince Albert's pencilled notes, included 'Doubtful – Conceit – Working for Himself' and 'Not fit from personal weakness'. Not one of them responded satisfactorily in the essays the Prince set them as part of the selection process.

Then came Edward White Benson, warmly endorsed by one of the country's leading educationalists and with a testimonial from Lord Derby's nephew, who had been taught by him at Rugby: 'He was much liked, for he has a very interesting way of talking and teaching, and was ever ready to explain any difficulty.' Benson was indeed academically brilliant, having taken a double first in classics and maths at Trinity College, Cambridge, and been awarded the Chancellor's Medal. It is a happy detail in the story that the Chancellor of Cambridge University was none other than the Prince Consort. There were worries, of course. As Queen Victoria confessed to the Dean of Windsor, 'the beloved Prince' was 'anxious ... that Wellington College should in no way become an Eton or Harrow'. She and her husband were undoubtedly correct in fearing that Benson 'leant that way'.

90 The College hall, now known as 'Old Hall', on South Front, 1859
Wellington College

So in March 1858 the 29-year-old assistant master from Rugby was appointed as Wellington College's first Headmaster. He was to stay for nearly 15 years. A salary of £800 per annum was agreed, plus a house and allowances. Benson was already engaged to his cousin, Mary Sidgwick, whom he married 15 months after taking up the post at Wellington. It may well be that an important reason for accepting the Headship, rather than returning to Cambridge (where he was a fellow of Trinity College), was that he wanted to get married. Only as Master of Wellington College could he get married and have accommodation provided for himself and his wife.

Temple had warned Governors that he 'did not think it possible to procure a good Headmaster for less than £800 a year'. In February 1860, just a year after the College opened, we find Benson complaining to Talbot:

91 A dormitory group, *c.*1867
Wellington College

92 Upper Middle II, with their master Henry Eve, 1861
Wellington College

93 The Leavers, 1867
Wellington College

94 The College prefects, 1867
Wellington College

The Headmaster's present salary of £800 is insufficient ... People are constantly coming – almost Daily – either to see their sons, and to see me about them at the same time – or to make enquiries & see the college with a view to sending children. In this hotel-less country I cannot send them away without luncheon, nor can I send them away from my house at luncheon time to obtain refreshments from the Steward.

In the solid material of mutton & beef, bread, sherry, and beer, I am really at very considerable expense. Upon the original plan of the college the headmaster might have been able to keep aloof. But now when boys come from higher classes and are considered to pay fairly for their education, visitors come direct to the headmaster and expect to be sustained as they are at other schools.

Head teachers today will find themselves agreeing with Benson's insistence that 'the market value of a headmaster's work is higher. The work itself is never over, and knows scarcely any leisure, or holiday'. Benson used as his gold standard Rugby School, whose Governors

95 The Common Room, 1867
Wellington College

'consider they cannot secure the service they want without providing £3,000 a year, and *all* the other great schools pay more.' Determined that Wellington College should join the ranks of the great schools, Benson carried his research further, citing the £1,250 a year paid to the Head of Marlborough, despite the College's £30,000 debt. He reminded Talbot that his own annual salary as an assistant master at Rugby had been in the region of £950 to £1,000, and, in deciding to head Wellington, he had turned down the offer of becoming a housemaster at Rugby: this post would have taken his pay up to 'at least £1,600 or £1,800 clear'.

Benson was indeed stupendously conscientious in carrying out his work. 'To him', states Talboys, 'life was an endless expansion of work; his vitality pervaded and encouraged the whole of the society in which he moved.' In this he bore some resemblance to the Duke of Wellington himself. Despite his anxieties about the personal expense incurred, he and his wife Mary – who was just 18 when she joined him at Wellington as his new bride – were generous hosts, inviting to the Master's Lodge not only distinguished academic and clerical visitors but also his Common

Room colleagues (see plate 95). Although a shy young woman by nature, Mary responded with enthusiasm to their many guests: 'What walks, what talks, what mirth!' Sometimes on summer evenings she arranged for their visitors' dinner to be laid out on a table on the Master's Lodge lawn. Occasionally she held séances. Theirs was a real family home (they moved to the Lodge in 1865 and its design was based on Benson's own plans) and in it were born their six children. It is recorded that, in the early days of the Headship at least, every evening after prayers Mrs Benson would shake hands with each boy and wish him good night. Later, after the family had moved into the Lodge, the pupils would have breakfast with the Headmaster, and sometimes tea with his children in the nursery. Mary's nickname became 'Mother Benjy'. She acted for years as her husband's only secretary and was evidently an object of much interest among the pupils. The rumour was that she smoked cigarettes on the roof while her husband – who deplored tobacco – was busy at school.

It was not only with regard to his own salary that Benson felt moved to write to the Governors. About a year after the College opened the Headmaster reported:

> *I am sorry to say that I have met with much difficulty in obtaining masters at £150 a year, which is all that can be offered to masters who are not also tutors of dormitories.*
>
> *In seeking a new master I have had 5 refusals in a fortnight from gentlemen who were likely to come, & I find that the salary has been the objection. There is just the difference which tells, between £150 and £200 a year – £200 is the value of many College fellowships, & this enters into the calculations of young men hesitating in their choice of work.*

Once again, we see Benson's ear to the ground, his criticisms placed in context and his understanding nothing if not pragmatic. He glimpsed the wider implications for the reputation of the College, of course: in an early report to the Governors Benson reminded them that 'one incompetent master will be enough seriously to injure the place.'

Benson found some success, at least, over the question of recruiting staff to teach additional subjects, Talbot informing him in March 1859: 'I am sure I do not know where the funds are to come from, but I suppose I must concede to your demands both with respect to the Drawing and other Masters who make periodical visits to the College.' The financial strain felt by the Governors is indicated by the rather bald suggestion that follows: 'I have always thought that you might make use of the Professors at Sandhurst who would not want travelling money.' Shortly before the College opened, Talbot asked Benson to 'remember we have not *one shilling* to spare' but as Wellington started to flourish, Benson

96 North Front before landscaping, 1859

Wellington College

The decorative wall and urns were subsequently removed to make way for the current driveway.

97 A scene of everyday life in Front Quad during the College's first year, 1859

Wellington College

98 Great School in its original configuration, 1859

Wellington College

secured an increase in salaries for teachers who, by September 1860, had become a staff of nine. It was agreed that Mr Wright, the senior assistant master, would live out of College. In the house to be built for him in 1861 boarders would pay a fee of £140. This arrangement helped to overcome a problem that continued to beset the young school: its original buildings had not been designed to accommodate the total pupil numbers needed to make the whole enterprise viable. It was the first of several Houses built on College land where the parents paid fees directly to the housemaster. These boys ate separately from those living in the 'in-College' Dormitories, to whom they generally considered themselves superior. This is how Houses such as the Stanley and the Benson came into being – set apart slightly from the main body of the College. The original Dormitories were packed together around Front and Back Quads. This was a felicitous way of matching each to the military leader – for example Lord Lynedoch and Sir George Murray – whose statues were placed in alcoves close by. The running of the Dormitories was by no means straightforward. Not long after the College opened, the matron, Mrs Booth, was dismissed. She had not been given the ideal preparation in caring for adolescent boys, her husband having run a convict settlement prior to their arrival at Wellington.

Although a man deeply engaged in the pursuit of the intellectual life, Benson possessed a keen practical bent and never considered beneath his notice the little things that can make daily life palatable – or their opposite. He advised the Governors as early as 1858, when the College was still a work in progress:

> *There seems to me to be one important omission in the present state of the buildings. That of a Bath. There is no stream near the place in which the scholars can bathe, and both for health's and comfort's sake boys should not be without the opportunity of doing so. If the excellent hot water arrangements could be applied so as to make the bath gently tepid when necessary (since a covered bath is always colder than one in the open air) it would be advantageous.*

99 Two 'original' Wellingtonians, J. Spence (L) and J. Boughey (R), 1859

Wellington College

Boughey was the first Head of College (Head Boy) and both became senior generals later in life. Now fully grown up they appear to have donned their original official uniforms, ten or twenty years later, unadapted (see plate 76, page 111).

Two years later, Benson's sharp eye picked up shortcomings in rather a different aspect of school life: 'It is with considerable reluctance that I write to you [Mr Bishop] again to express that the state of the stationery cupboards is highly unsatisfactory to me.' He goes on to explain his objections:

> *Neatness is essential for the sake of accuracy in any branch of business and this is business though on a small scale. But it is also still more incumbent to have this portion well arranged as a pattern to the boys of*

what their own arrangements should resemble. It is vain to expect orderliness from them in their books and papers, when our own stores of those things, – so important a part of the College economy – are thus untidy and disorderly.

Benson is here shown to be consistent and logical, his principles extending to all aspects of College life, however mundane. He was able to grasp the inter-connectedness of things, especially where boarding school education is concerned.

Writing to architect John Shaw in 1858, Benson had included his own drawings showing what he believed to be the ideal 'learning desks' for the Great School classroom. A brilliant mathematician, he was able to calculate that these desks and their benches would be eight and a half feet long:

> *I think that I should like even the desks and benches which run lengthwise of the school to be moveable, at least the two lowest tiers ... These desks, which I will call saying desks, meaning Desks for saying lessons at, ... which I propose to place transversely, opposite to the master's desks, in lieu of the semi-circular seats may be of the simplest kind. At Rugby we have them made only like tall benches, so that a saying bench and desk appear thus in section.* [Here he includes the diagram he has drawn]; *the desks are wanted by all but the least boys in taking notes.*

It is striking that long before educationalists recognised the importance of classroom furniture (such as the Harkness Table, which is used at Wellington College today) Benson was up to the mark and thinking ahead.

In his letter to Shaw, Benson waxed eloquent and inventive on the 'drawing desks', advising that:

> *In one of the schools* [meaning 'subject rooms'] *there ought to be a contrivance for fixing frames up on the desks in order to support patterns for drawing, and the seats ought to be capable of being removed with ease (perhaps the benches should be shorter here) so as to be suited to the light, and so as to give a boy plenty of space (as he may require it) for his drawing board.*

In another diagram Benson marked where the master's seat should be placed – 'and in order that no corner may be out of his sight perhaps the Book Closet should be at B' – and he included a drawn plan of precisely how the classroom should be laid out. Benson was not being stubbornly prescriptive here: he knew perfectly well, as did the architect and the Governors, that he was the one with the practical experience needed to design the new school.

Shortly afterwards, in April 1858, we find Benson writing again to Shaw, criticising the architect's plan to design desks:

> *open in front, with the top fixed. This appears to me to be objectionable on the ground of the difficulty of cleaning out; if a boy upsets an ink-pot inside, the ink will run, ... spreading about among his books and papers which he will be vainly groping to find out where the mischief is. The dust will also accumulate in the corners and be difficult to get rid of: the desk cannot be opened at any moment to the master's eye; forbidden articles may easily be concealed in them, and thorough neatness will be very difficult to enforce.*

You could call this obsessive, or you might choose to salute Benson's minute grasp of what goes on in classrooms. He was ready to suggest

100 The bust of Wellington and the motto of the Wellesley family, which translates as 'Fortune is the companion of virtue', preside over Remembrance Day ceremonies in Front Quad, 2013

models on which Wellington's classroom furniture might be based: 'there is a very beautifully arranged desk of very simple construction which is used for 250 boys in the Great Classical School in King Edward's School at Birmingham.' He adds, rather touchingly, 'I have never seen any desk which I like so well or think so suitable to a boy's use.' One might even describe this as an early example of child-centred learning, Benson placing as much, if not more, emphasis on the needs of the pupils than the convenience of his staff.

His thoughts turning to the 'Boys' library', Benson hoped that the Governors 'will be disposed to grant some small annual allowance for the purchase of books ... Some books of reference are already much required, and the works of most of our standard authors, as well as books of history, biography, and travels ought to be placed within their reach.' He complained that the library was 'of insufficient size, and is often crowded and unwholesome. The Building of a Library of convenient size, into which all books could be removed, both those which belong to the Masters and have been presented by them would solve both difficulties.' He was even prepared to ask his staff to make sacrifices for the sake of their charges: 'If the Masters thus resigned the use of the room now appropriated to them, that with the boys' library would give the two class rooms which we need.' At one point they were reduced to holding lessons in the Surgery and Surgery Kitchen.

So Benson was indeed a man with a vision and with imagination, which went far beyond dry educational philosophy. For example, he suggested they create 'a broad gallery at one end of the proposed new library'. This would 'give the masters almost as much privacy as at present, and their presence would make it easier for the librarians to preserve quiet among the boys'. His vision succeeded in marrying the aesthetic with the practical.

Young but experienced, Benson was always alert to potential hazards. 'I have just ascertained', he informed the Governors, 'that boys find no difficulty in climbing up and down out of the balconies at the ends of the lower dormitories. This will lead to mischief, and it is necessary to introduce some means by which the exit and entrance can be effectively prevented at night.' His views on discipline match his characteristic blend of idealism and pragmatism. Even in the middle of the nineteenth century a school's image with the public was recognised as crucial:

> *In the case of some serious offences committed by young boys it is desirable to avoid publicity and exposure as far as possible – While it is essential that he should leave his school and companions both for their sake and his own, the one hope for a boy in his subsequent career often lies in his being able to make a new start.*

Characteristically, Benson showed sensitivity in understanding the needs of both the College and the families affected: 'In these cases I wish to know whether (1) parents may be allowed to remove their boys by giving notice to the Secretary as in other cases, or (2) it is necessary for the headmaster to inform the Governors of the cause of removal.' Benson had done his research: 'I believe that the first of these alternatives is the practice in other public schools, as the only course by which degradation consequent on exposure can be really avoided.'

Benson always had his ear to the ground, following each pupil's development with a keen personal interest. He caned those who produced shoddy work, practising discipline with the help of his prefects and using the system he had seen successfully adopted at Rugby. He discouraged fagging, but it was perhaps inevitable that many of the younger boys found themselves acting as the prefects' servants (see plate 94). The prefects were allowed to issue corporal punishment and entitled to deliver up to six blows, while the Head of College could ratchet up a total of ten should he so choose.

Benson lived according to the principles he had refined, and in leading Wellington College from its inception, he saw a means of putting these into practice. In a letter to Talbot he declared:

> *In forming the School of Wellington College, and in developing its principles of management and moral discipline, I have always acted upon the belief that there are two evils which must, above all others, be guarded against ...: untruthfulness, and indecency with its consequent mischiefs ... Wellington is yet free from bad traditions; I believe we have every opportunity of keeping it pure.*

Benson's firm ethical line on the boys' behaviour was surpassed by his educational philosophy. He was quite clear about the curriculum: this was to be an academic school. A year before the school opened he was advising Talbot that they needed to admit:

> *a certain number of Elder Boys ... The difference between the age of 16 and that at which the University man enters life, (22 or 23) is very great ... The year between 16 and 17 is also generally considered in Schools as a very important year in a Boy's progress; I have spoken to several of the best masters in England who agree in stating this. For the rest of the School it is also desirable that Boys of diligence and influential character should remain as long as possible. No one can estimate, except those who have seen it, the power for good which such Boys exert upon their fellows.*

Benson planned that able and ambitious boys entering the school aged 14 or 15 should begin their term a week earlier than their younger fellows, so that they might develop a rapport with their teachers and be primed as to 'the responsibility which would rest on them as leading Boys in the school'. So, as long ago as the mid-nineteenth century the Master of Wellington was promoting the concept of a 'gifted and talented' stream.

In advocating the admission of older boys to the College, he set a high entry bar:

> *A thorough knowledge of Arithmetic including Decimal Fractions, the first Book of Euclid, and a fair acquaintance with Latin will be required. Weight will be attached to good examination passes in French, German, History, or any branch of Natural or Experimental Philosophy in which candidates may wish to be examined. But superficial knowledge of these subjects will not be held of any value.*

Not surprisingly it was concerning Latin that he was at his most prescriptive: 'a boy must be able to construe Caesar or Virgil and translate a simple passage of English into Latin Prose correctly by the help of a Dictionary'.

In his bid to raise the academic profile of the fledgling school, Benson suggested that a class should be specifically created for boys intending to go to university. This, he argued, would benefit the Foundationers, 'whose experience at home is of the narrowest'. His vision was for all pupils to learn Latin; Greek and German would also be introduced, the latter to be compulsory. In this he found a champion in Lord Derby, who favoured strong ties with the universities. The Governors could not find it in them, however, to follow Benson's plan of sponsoring a special Exhibition of £50 per annum for four years – or rather, they could not find the cash.

Of the 76 boys who were there when the College opened in January 1859, 47 were Foundationers. As the criterion for admission was their status as officers' orphans rather than academic prowess, many of them had been quite poorly educated up to that point. Benson objected to the way Foundationers were selected, with a committee of Governors using relative poverty as the chief criterion, rather than academic potential. But in appointing Benson the Governors secured a Headmaster whose strong links with Cambridge, and with some of the country's top private schools, would prove enormously beneficial to the more intellectually aspiring of his pupils. He could see that a larger number of boys would wish to enrol at Wellington if they saw it as a route to university. 'By cutting off University prospects it appears to me', he complained, 'that Wellington College would reject many of those whom it would most wish to help, namely the cleverest and the most ambitious sons of poor officers.' Of course Wellingtonians would proceed to the military academies at Sandhurst and Woolwich, but it was Benson's legacy that saw many others choosing Oxford or Cambridge University instead. But it was not easy. Benson complained how very difficult he found it:

> *to excite any really liberal interest in literature or arts in the minds of boys who are aware that in one or two years they will have to pass examinations such as are required of the army or other services ... The presence of a class intended for the universities, having really liberal studies to pursue, in a wide spirit, not by 'cram-books', and with abundant time before them, is what we want in order to diffuse a really cultivated and thoughtful tone of mind in the school.*

He believed it was 'of great importance that people should know that we do not take a second rate position as to the style of education given. I am now asked scarcely any question so often as "Will your education do for boys proceeding to the university?".'

Benson understood that in creating the desired ethos, the smallest of details could prove critical. Therefore, he frowned on handing books out 'gratuitously' to the pupils, for it would 'lead to carelessness and ill usage of the books – and the boys will be able to take no pride in their well-ordered little library'. He attached importance to the daily timetable: when the school first opened weekdays began at 6.30am (although Benson later allowed this to be pushed back by half an hour), with lessons all morning – and, of course, a Chapel service. Afternoon lessons continued until 3.15pm callover (registration). After a 6.15pm tea, the boys worked in Great School on their supervised prep. The day closed with evening Chapel.

His Christian faith lay at the heart of everything Benson did. Accepting his appointment as Wellington College's first leader, he confided to his friend Joseph Barber Lightfoot that God's hand 'seems to place me where His Spirit, as I trust, teaches me I must be'. Eventually that place was to be the new cathedral in Truro and to culminate in Canterbury in 1883. He loved hymns, overseeing the 1860 edition of *Wellington College Chapel Hymns*, all of which had been chosen by Benson himself, and several translated by him from the Latin. Throughout his life Benson continued to use this hymnal in his private chapel. During his time at Wellington he found himself having to explain his position, assuring Lady Havelock in 1860 that 'Any report of High Church teaching in this place is unfounded ... I hold that the first religious duty to boys is to try to make them simply wise and good and conscientious.' He did not force the children of Dissenters to attend Chapel services, although he worried that this could mean they grew up 'indifferent to the paramount duty of united religious worship with their fellow Christians'. A month after the College opened Benson expressed his concerns about a Roman

Catholic pupil whose mother had forbidden him from attending services or religion classes at Wellington. Benson's Christianity was broad and inclusive: what he wanted for his young charges was the meaning and the depth that religion could bring into their lives. His spirituality went beyond religious denomination. Although, according to Talboys, 'His wrath was terrible', he found the stillness of his God in the beauties of Creation. His favourite walk was the Finchampstead Ridges, where he listened to 'the wind murmuring like the sea in the heavily tressed branches above. Within the wood near Edgebarrow was an avenue of long spruce first called by him the "Eternal Calm", ... for on the windiest days it was peaceful there.'

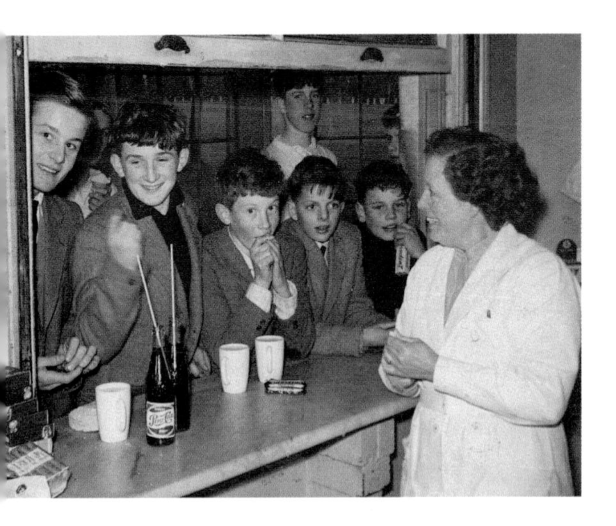

101 Wellingtonians partaking at 'Grubbies', the College tuck shop, *c.*1955
Wellington College

102 The annual Kingsleys Run sees Wellingtonians brave frigid lake waters to reach the finish line, 2014

Early life at Wellington took other turns as well, with sport always an important part of each week. The College, built from scratch on moorland, had no sports pitches. The boys had to dig with bare hands and turf the First Eleven's pitch. Instead of 'Grubbies' (the tuck shop), 'the Honeywoman's Cottage' offered tea and basic treats (see plate 101). Charles Kingsley, rector at Eversley, invented the Kingsleys Run, which originally required Wellingtonians to wade across the River Blackwater area (see plate 102). Kingsley also championed football at Wellington, as well as paper-chasing, in which 'hares' left a paper trail for other runners to follow. 'I watched the running of your boys on Saturday', Kingsley wrote to Benson. 'As for pluck, I never saw boys more determined or cheerful at their work, which in the large water meadows was very hard.' Relations with the College's other neighbours, at Sandhurst, were occasionally strained. Benson wrote in February 1859 to complain to the Governor, Sir Harry Jones, about 50 or 60 cadets who 'came over here' at the weekend 'and made themselves free of our college while we were at divine service. Some penetrated the kitchens, ... some climbed the walls round the gardens, and made a great noise shouting, and as I am informed using improper language'.

One of Benson's most important early tasks was to plan the College's first Speech Day, set for summer 1860. The Prince Consort intended to donate a prize for an English Historical Essay, and Lord Derby one for French, while the Archbishop of Canterbury was offering one for Theological Studies. It was in the initial correspondence on this topic in May 1859 that the Queen's plan to award a Gold Medal as a 'good Conduct Prize' was announced. Benson drew up a list of annual competitive prizes, including translations into Latin, German and French, and for Chemistry, Botany, Mathematics and Religious Studies. Benson's suggestion was that the value of the prizes be increased by funding from the Governors: 'If H.R.H., the President, or if any of the individual Governors, or the Vice-President, would bestow any of the above prizes it would give a distinctive character to such prizes which would be very effective as a stimulus to exertion.' He also envisaged Form Prizes, the largest number to be awarded in the Fifth Form, calculating the cost at £23.

As always, Benson's plans were meticulous. He drew a diagram showing where everyone would sit on Speech Day, including chairs on the dais for the Governors and 'distinguished visitors', and another diagram of the coat of arms and wording, as they should appear inside the prize books – for example, 'PRIZE FOR DIVINITY GIVEN BY THE ARCHBISHOP OF CANTERBURY'. Below this on his diagram appears the Duke's coat of arms and the date. Benson was unsurprisingly prescriptive about the choice of books to be given as prizes, while Lord Derby preferred to let the prize winners make their own choice, 'to the value of £5'.

Prince Albert planned to attend Speech Day, but would not take part in the proceedings and would have to return to Osborne by dinner time, 'so his stay will necessarily be a little circumscribed'. The day was deemed a great success, with Lord Derby writing to congratulate Benson on 2 August 1860: 'I was particularly pleased with the appearance of all the boys, and more especially the generality of the Prize recipients. I am glad to hear that a large proportion of the latter were Foundationers. Could you give me their names?' He took pride in 'the condition and prospects of what I hope I may live to see one of the foremost of our public Schools'.

Benson's first Head of College was John Boughey, who was awarded the Queen's Medal at Speech Day (see plate 99). Although the Queen was unable to give it in person, she had strong views on the criteria: 'The Queen gives a Medal to the boy of the finest and most noble character in

The College ... and the qualities which gain this medal should, if possible, be characterized in the Inscription upon it.' Prince Albert, she assured him, was keen to consult with Benson on the subject. On 28 July 1860 Benson justified his choice in a letter to the Prince Consort's secretary:

> *The name which I mentioned to the Prefects was that of Boughey, and it has been received with great satisfaction. I think it right to add, as His Royal Highness will probably wish to know how the election went off, that I had determined after consultation with the masters to propose the name of a boy no way remarkable for cleverness but supposed most exemplary for conduct.*

On consulting the prefects he 'found ... that there was scarcely a difference of opinion among them as to the remarkable merits of Boughey in not only organizing the prefects for their duty, and inspiriting them to be firm, but also in the great matters of kindness and protection of the younger boys'. It is in his choice of Boughey, through consultative democracy, with the rigorous academic making way for the Christian who recognised development of character as the mainstay of a truly great education, that we see Benson at his finest. We also see the convergence in educational philosophy of Wellington College's first Master and the idealistic Prince Consort.

103 The Dining Hall at Wellington College, 2013
Notice the House banners suspended from the walls.

CHAPTER V

The Chapel

104 The Chapel of the Holy Spirit at Wellington College, 2014

When Wellington College first opened, the Chapel was a stuffy little space in the Orange House reached by a daunting stone staircase. It was only when Governors agreed in 1860 that the building of a Chapel should be funded from capital and also, as the College itself had been, by public subscription, that Benson and the Prince Consort were able to move forward on the project. Benson complained that Prince Albert laughed when he suggested that raising subscriptions would be easy. The laying of the foundation stone on 12 July 1861 coincided with the College's second Speech Day. As the *Daily Telegraph* reported the following day:

> *The distribution of prizes took place in the great hall, the Head Master ... occupying the chair, while on his right sat his Royal Highness the Prince Consort ... Mr Spence, major, was called up as the successful candidate for the high honour of the Queen's ... Medal ... His Royal Highness complimented Mr Spence on the ability and industry he had displayed, and presented him with the medal amidst loud applause.*

The Prince Consort appears to have taken a more active role than he had at the College's first Speech Day a year earlier when John Boughey had been awarded the medal. Later that morning he laid the Chapel's foundation stone at a special ceremony, processing in to the singing of Psalm 122 – 'I was glad when they said unto me: we will go into the house of the Lord'. The Prince, according to Benson, had 'made divers awful propositions', notably that the Chapel should be an exact but smaller version of Eton's, built from brick. His last contact with Wellington was a meeting in November 1861, where he supported Benson's proposed alterations to the Chapel.

105 An illustration of the College Chapel produced for an architecture periodical, 1861

Wellington College

Less than five months after presiding over Speech Day and laying the foundation stone, Albert was dead. He was probably a victim of typhoid fever, Windsor's drainage and sewerage being notoriously poor. From the moment he died on 16 December 1861 Queen Victoria went into mourning for 40 years. Apparently she burst into tears when, in 1864, she was shown the Chapel's foundation stone. 'O Blameless Prince', wrote Benson in his scrapbook, 'and stainless gentleman'. In his letter of condolence to the Queen, Lord Derby observed: 'Among the Institutions which will have to deplore the Prince's loss, the Wellington College will not have the least cause. It has mainly risen to its present position through his constant superintendence and encouragement, and we shall grievously miss his fostering hand, his liberal assistance and his judicious advice.' Immediately, those visits from Prince Albert, and the genuine interest he had always taken in the College, seemed irreplaceable. Near the Chapel entrance the oak stalls bearing Albert's crest are his memorial.

But with the Prince Consort gone, Benson could at least focus without royal interference on his own personal vision for the Chapel's design. For him, this project was more important than completing the Dormitories. It is appropriate that later, as Bishop of the newly created Truro see,

Benson built England's first gothic cathedral since the Middle Ages. At Wellington he envisaged an edifice that, although criticised by a later Master and historian of the College, David Newsome, as 'not satisfactory', and certainly one that rises somewhat incongruously from John Shaw's 'Wrenaissance' structure, is undoubtedly a classic example of Victorian gothic architecture (see plate 109). He took pride in having rescued the Chapel from being a 'frightful and indestructible meeting house'. Its spire was modelled on that of Sainte Chapelle in Paris. A contemporary newspaper account describes it as 'a simple parallelogram, with a semicircular east end. It is divided by massive buttresses into five bays'. The Chapel was connected to the College buildings by the Chapel Arch, designed to weld seamlessly the two different styles (see plate 112). Benson's favourite part was the Ante-chapel arch, which features squirrels and birds. He was especially keen that details of the interior design should blend with the countryside around Wellington that he had already grown to love. Thus stone carvings feature local flowers and leaves, ferns and pines – and of course the ubiquitous squirrel. It is said that the stonemasons scoured the neighbourhood during their lunch break in search of local flora.

As prescriptive in dictating the minutiae of Chapel design as he had been over the construction and layout of desks, Benson suggested – in a letter preserved in his scrapbook – that:

106 Original design for the Chapel rose window by the Parisian glaziers Lusson, *c.*1859
Wellington College

107 George Gilbert Scott (1811–1878)
Original drawing for the Chapel window frames, *c.*1859
Wellington College

108 Original designs for the Chapel chancel windows by the Parisian glaziers Lusson, *c*.1859

Wellington College

These windows were destroyed in the Second World War.

The size of the foliage seems to be so small that it would be a pity to attempt too much, or too great variety, for fear of confusing it ... I think therefore that it will be best to keep as much as possible to the Rose both in flower, leaves & fruit – since this is the Royal English flower & will suit the material ... If the Rose flower is used at the angles of the principal caps, it would give a sort of connection in style with the capitals throughout the building – Roses again (not necessarily Tudor Roses) might appear in the rafters, and rose leaves along the cornice.

109 The College Chapel, as completed, 1860s

Wellington College

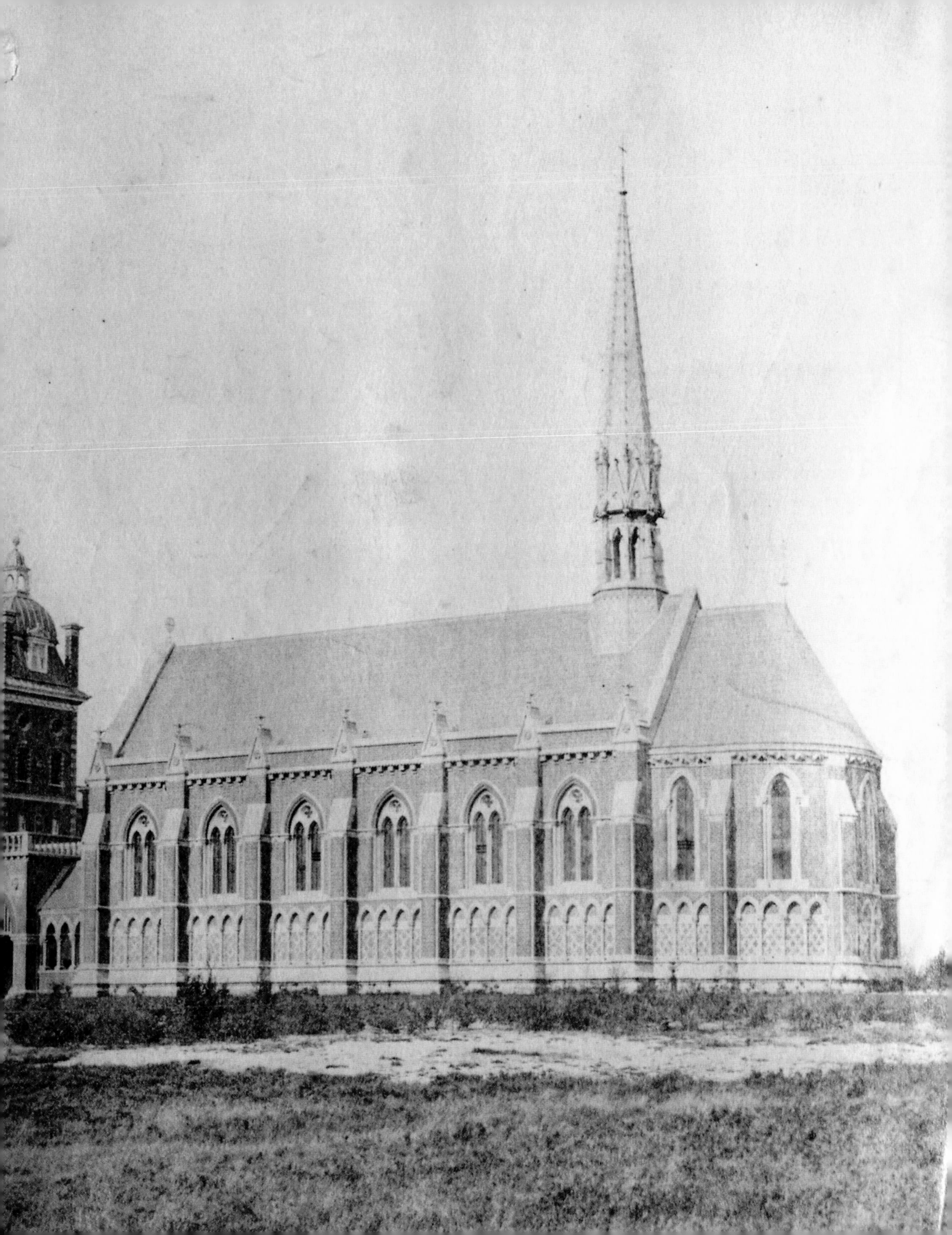

110 George Gilbert Scott (1811–1878)
Original drawing for the Chapel chancel, *c.*1859
Wellington College

111 Detail from the Chapel stained-glass windows, 2012

The scrapbook contains Benson's handwritten list of plants that he would like featured in the decoration, for example columbine, maple, dog rose, water lily, poppy, hop, primrose, heather, buttercup and ivy. On a plan of the nave Benson marked by hand where each featured flower should appear.

Benson paid equally minute attention to the arrangement of the pews:

> *The boys sit according to dormitories, of about 30 boys, and the benches should accordingly hold 10, 15 or 30 boys each, so that the dormitories may be regularly divided & sit together ... The back row of seats to be raised 2 steps, the second 1, the lowest to be on the floor ... The 2 steps to the masters' stalls to be higher ... so as to place them 3 or 4 inches higher than the rest.*

Any potential problem Benson was ready to forestall: 'To avoid pretexts for lounging it is desirable to make the book boards as low as possible, and the space between book board & seat as wide as possible – our personal measurements are 19 inches is allowed [*sic*] to each boy.'

The original building, consisting of a single central aisle, with inward-facing tiered pews, was much narrower than today's (see plate 115). It was enlarged in 1886, proving Benson correct in his warning (in an 1861 letter pasted into the scrapbook) that the mere 300 seats in the original plan would be inadequate should pupil numbers grow: 'To add 18 feet to length and 6 to width will not cost much now, but hereafter, the appreciation of 10 times this amount will leave it a botched building.' The architect, George Gilbert Scott (see plate 110), a master of the Victorian gothic, also designed the Albert Memorial in Kensington. Benson's scrapbook shows evidence of a disagreement between Headmaster and architect, notably over when a porch becomes an Ante-chapel. Scott's objections to Benson's demands for an Ante-chapel arose chiefly 'as a matter of taste'. Apologising for what had evidently been construed as criticism, Benson tactfully re-invented his proposed Ante-chapel as 'a closed Porch', which, he explained, would be 'more convenient for our purposes than an open one'. Once again, practical considerations dictated his thinking: 'It will be difficult to prevent little boys from making it a play place ... At night too especially in our gipsy neighbourhood I should not like to have such a place open.'

Scott's Chapel, completed to Benson's satisfaction and indeed with his own stamp marking every aspect of its design, was dedicated on 16 July 1863. At the bottom of the service booklet preserved in Benson's

112 South Front and the Chapel before landscaping, *c.*1870
Wellington College

scrapbook Lord Derby has written 'Noble language indeed', and added his signature. The collection at the end of the service was 'devoted to the Decoration of the Chapel with Stained Glass Windows' – another of Benson's projects (see plate 111). Like the laying of the foundation stone two years earlier, the ceremony coincided with the College Speech Day. The preacher was Samuel Wilberforce, Bishop of Oxford and son of Abolitionist William. The advice to Wellingtonians at the heart of his sermon was 'Learn how to live'.

This is what the pupils of Wellington College have always done. The institution founded in memory of the great Duke continues to keep to Prince Albert's principle of educating the child for life. The Duke of Wellington grew into the victor of Waterloo, Prime Minister, and a man who despite strains in his personal life discovered how to find his own inner peace. All this could not have been achieved if he had not learned how to live. His model serves as a lasting legacy to the young people who pass through the gates marked 'Heroum Filii' (Sons of heroes).

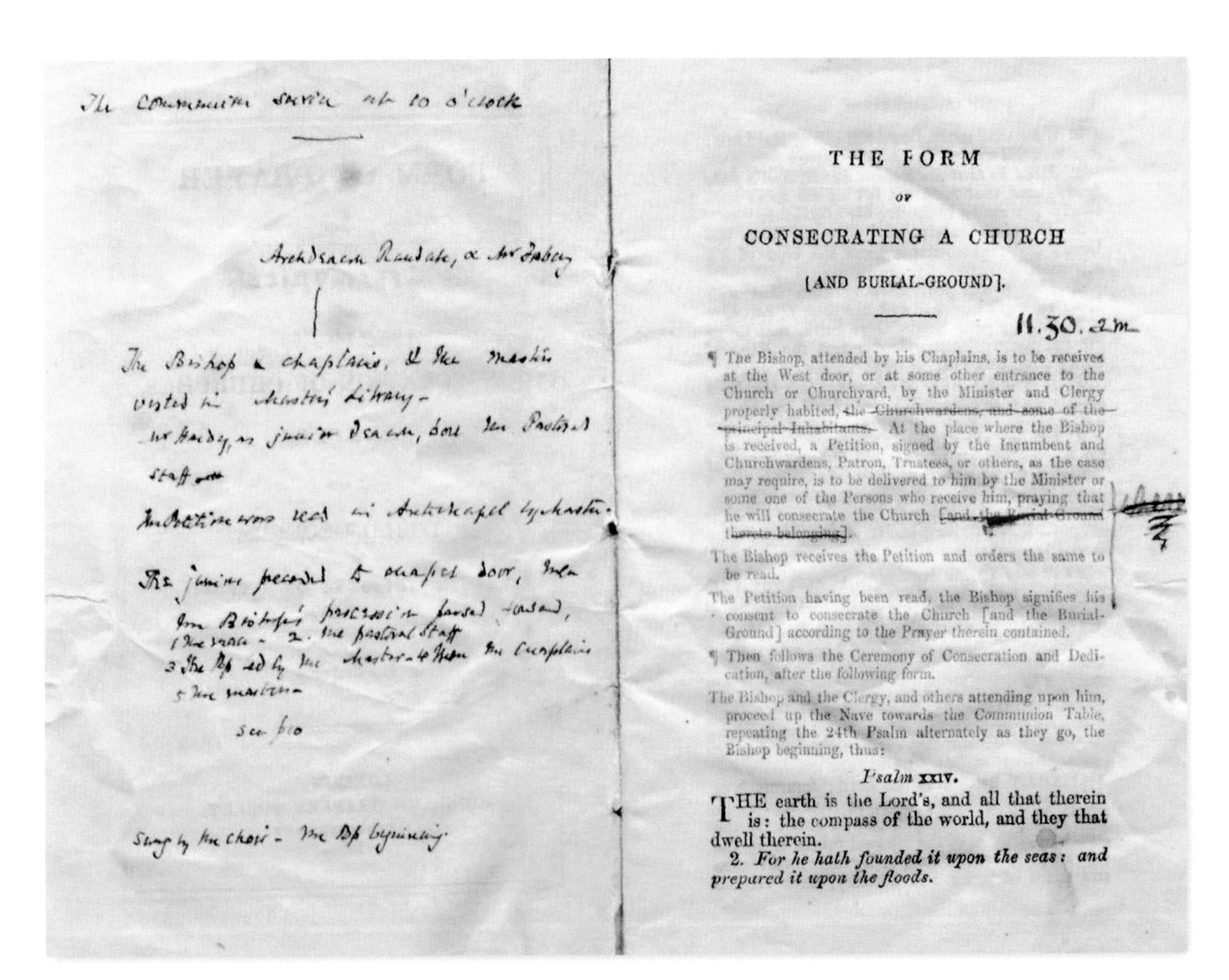

THE FORM

OF

CONSECRATING A CHURCH

[AND BURIAL-GROUND].

11.30. a.m.

¶ The Bishop, attended by his Chaplains, is to be received at the West door, or at some other entrance to the Church or Churchyard, by the Minister and Clergy properly habited, ~~the Churchwardens, and some of the principal Inhabitants.~~ At the place where the Bishop is received, a Petition, signed by the Incumbent and Churchwardens, Patron, Trustees, or others, as the case may require, is to be delivered to him by the Minister or some one of the Persons who receive him, praying that he will consecrate the Church ~~[and the Burial-Ground thereto belonging]~~.

The Bishop receives the Petition and orders the same to be read.

The Petition having been read, the Bishop signifies his consent to consecrate the Church [and the Burial-Ground] according to the Prayer therein contained.

¶ Then follows the Ceremony of Consecration and Dedication, after the following form.

The Bishop and the Clergy, and others attending upon him, proceed up the Nave towards the Communion Table, repeating the 24th Psalm alternately as they go, the Bishop beginning, thus:

Psalm xxiv.

THE earth is the Lord's, and all that therein is: the compass of the world, and they that dwell therein.

2. *For he hath founded it upon the seas: and prepared it upon the floods.*

113 Annotated Order of Service from the consecration of the College Chapel, 1861
Wellington College

114 Graduating Wellingtonians, 2013

Loyalty and fellowship continue to define Wellington's pupils as they have from the earliest days of the College.

overleaf

115 Matriculation of new Third Form pupils in the Chapel, 2014

With their backs towards us are Heads of College Nicky Maxwell (L) and Emily Curtis (centre right), and 13th Master Sir Anthony Seldon (R).

Wellington College Today

Independent School of the Year 2014

Top IB School in Britain 2014 *The Times*

Most Innovative School in Britain 2014 *Tatler*

Top Rugby School in Britain 2014 *Daily Mail*

Arts Council Gold Award for National Quality Arts Provision

Most Improved School at A Level in Britain (up from 256th to 21st, 2006–14) *Sunday Times*

116 The Wellington Academy, Ludgershall, Wiltshire, 2011

Founded in 2009, the Wellington Academy is a non-selective state-funded academy school educating pupils aged 11–19.

117 Wellington College Shanghai, 2013

The newest Wellington international school brings the educational ethos and experience of Wellington College to mainland China.

118 Wellingtonians participate in the annual Boughey Run, 2012

Commemorating the first Head of College, the objective is to run from Great Gate to Swan Lake and back before the clock finishes striking noon.

119 A dance performance in Combermere Quad, 2012

The architecture of the College's open spaces continues to promote community life.

In Memoriam

To the memory of Arthur Valerian Wellesley, 8th Duke of Wellington (1915-2014), who passed away on 31 December 2014, aged 99, as this book was in the final stages of preparation. An inspirational descendant of the 1st Duke, he remained always a loyal friend to Wellington College.

The 8th Duke of Wellington greets members of Common Room during a visit to the College, 2009

Select Bibliography

PRIMARY DOCUMENTARY SOURCES

The Archive Collection at Wellington College

The National Archives, Kew

The Wellington Papers, Archives and Manuscripts Section, University of Southampton Library

SECONDARY SOURCES

Alphabetical List of Subscribers to a Memorial of the Duke of Wellington (London: Spottiswoode, Her Majesty's Stationery Office, 1857)

Benson, Arthur Christopher, *The Life of Edward White Benson*, Volume I (London: Macmillan, 1901)

Bolitho, Hector, *Albert the Good* (London: Cobden-Sanderson, 1933)

Bolitho, Hector (ed.), *The Prince Consort and His Brother: Two Hundred New Letters*, (London: Cobden-Sanderson, 1933)

Bolt, Rodney, *As Good as God, as Clever as the Devil: The Impossible Life of Mary Benson* (London: Atlantic Books, 2011)

Fitchett, W.H. (ed.), *Wellington's Men: Some Soldier Autobiographies* (London: Smith, Elder & Co., 1900)

Guedalla, Philip, *The Duke* (London: Hodder & Stoughton, 1931; 1937)

Hibbert, Christopher, *Wellington: A Personal History* (London: Harper Collins, 1997)

Holmes, Richard, *Wellington: The Iron Duke* (London: Harper Collins, 2003; 2007)

Holyoake, Gregory, *Wellington at Walmer* (Dover: Buckland Publications, 1996)

Howard, Sir Michael, *Waterloo* (Old Wellingtonian Society, 2014)

Longford, Elizabeth, *Wellington: The Years of the Sword* (London: Weidenfeld & Nicolson, 1969)

Longford, Elizabeth, *Wellington: Pillar of State* (London: Weidenfeld & Nicolson, 1972)

Maxwell, W.H., *Life of the Duke of Wellington* (Edinburgh: W.P. Nimmo, Hay & Mitchell, 1898)

Mileham, Patrick, *Wellington College: The First 150 Years* (London: Third Millennium, 2008)

Mileham, Patrick, *Chapel of the Holy Spirit* (London: Wellington College and Third Millennium, 2011)

Newsome, David, *A History of Wellington College 1859–1959* (London: John Murray, 1959)

Paxman, Jeremy, *The Victorians: Britain Through the Paintings of the Age* (London: BBC Books, 2009)

Rappaport, Helen, *Magnificent Obsession: Victoria, Albert and the Death that Changed the Monarchy* (London: Hutchinson, 2011)

Snow, Peter, *To War with Wellington: From the Peninsula to Waterloo* (London: John Murray, 2010)

Talbot, W.P., *Narrative of the Foundation of Wellington College, Compiled by Direction of the Governors* (London: Harrison & Sons, 1874)

Talboys, R. St C., *A Victorian School: Being the Story of Wellington College* (Oxford: Blackwell, 1943)

Weller, Jac, *Wellington in the Peninsula 1808–1814* (London: Nicholas Vane, 1962)

Wellesley, Charles, Marquess of Douro, *Wellington Portrayed* (London: Unicorn Press, 2014)

Wellesley, Jane, *Wellington: A Journey Through My Family* (London: Weidenfeld & Nicolson, 2008)

Wilson, A.N., *The Victorians* (London: Hutchinson, 2002)

Photographic Credits

Pages 2, 20, 22, 26, 30, 32–33, 35, 46, 51, 57, 59, 67–68, 77, 98, 105 (bottom): © Bridgeman Images, London

Pages 4–5, 103, 117, 119, 121, 154 (right), 158–9 and back jacket: Photo: Joshua Moses © Wellington College Archives

Page 8: Photo: Dennis Johnson © Wellington College Archives

Pages 10, 64, 66, 74, 81, 94, 96, 102 (top left and bottom), 104, 108, 127: © Getty Images

Pages 16, 24 (top), 105 (top), 110 (top and bottom): © Victoria and Albert Museum, London

Pages 19, 34, 44, 69, 93: © English Heritage

Pages 24 (bottom), 55, 62, 85, 89: © Stratfield Saye Preservation Trust

Page 27: © UK Government Art Collection

Page 28: By permission of the Trustees of the Goodwood Collection

Page 29: © National Museums Liverpool

Pages 31, 42, 45, 48–50: © Council of the Army Museum, London

Pages 36, 70, 106, 112 and front jacket: Royal Collection Trust/© Her Majesty Queen Elizabeth II 2014

Pages 37 (left), 58, 72, 79, 82, 97, 102 (top right): © National Portrait Gallery, London

Page 37 (right): © RMN-Grand Palais (Musée d'Orsay)/Hervé Lewandowski

Page 38–39, 71, 92: © Tate, London 2014

Page 40: © The McGill University Napoleon Collection

Page 41: Photo: D. Bosquet © SPW-DGO4-Patrimoine

Page 54: The RAMC Muniment Collection in the care of the Wellcome Library, Wellcome Images

Page 61: Photo: John Gay © English Heritage

Page 86–87: Photo: Lewis Hulbert

Page 90: By permission of the Trustees of the Middlesex Guildhall Art Collection Trust

Pages 100, 107: © Wellington College Collection

Pages 111, 118, 123, 126, 128, 130–32, 133 (top, middle and bottom), 134–35, 137 (top, middle and bottom), 138, 145 (left), 148, 150, 151 (left and right), 152–53, 154 (left), 155–56: © Wellington College Archives

Pages 124–25: Photo: Joshua Moses © Wellington College Collection

Pages 140–41, 145 (right), 147, 157, 160 (bottom), 161 (top and bottom): Photo: Graeme Kennedy © Wellington College Archives

Page 160 (top): Photo: Building Design © Wellington College Archives

Page 162: Photo: © Ian Jones, 2009

Index